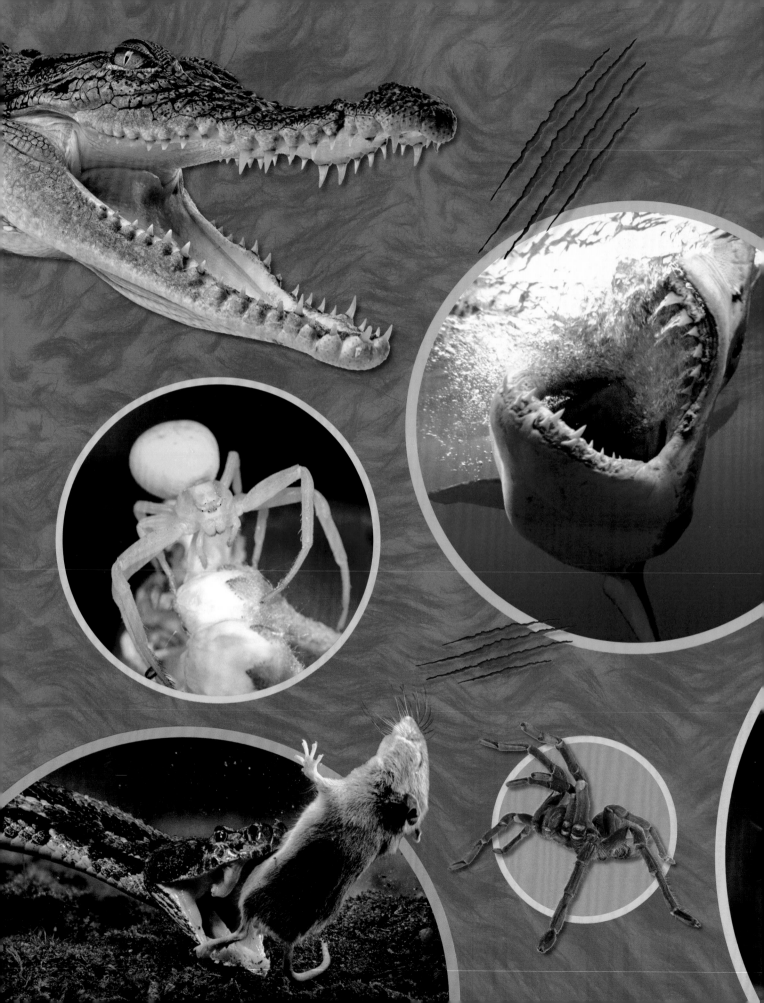

ULTIMATE PREDATOR-PEDIA

THE **MOST**
COMPLETE
PREDATOR
REFERENCE
EVER

**CHRISTINA
WILSDON**

NATIONAL GEOGRAPHIC
WASHINGTON, D.C.

TABLE OF CONTENTS

INTRODUCTION

PREDATORS ARE ANIMALS THAT KILL AND EAT OTHER ANIMALS.

I've got two of them living right inside my house!

You probably won't be surprised to learn that those two predators are a cat and a dog. Of course, they no longer need to prey on other animals to get the food they need. But their distant relatives in the wild do. In fact, two of those "cousins" prowl my neighborhood not far from Seattle—a big city in the state of Washington. At night, we hear coyotes yipping, and sometimes we glimpse a bobcat slipping through the woods.

These predators are all mammals, but the world of predators also includes reptiles, birds, fish, and all other groups of animals. Some predators are enormous, such as the blue whales that gulp down tons of thumb-size creatures for their meals. Some predators are so small that a drop of water is a

universe to them. A predatory "water bear" or tardigrade, for example, is no bigger than a poppy seed. An even smaller tardigrade could fit inside the period at the end of this sentence.

In the pages of *Ultimate Predatorpedia,* you'll meet some of the world's most famous predators, such as Bengal tigers, African lions, and great white sharks. You'll also meet small but determined predators, such as the larvae of insects called ant lions that build traps in the sand to snare their prey. And you'll find out about the amazing adaptations predators use to catch the food they need to survive.

These adaptations include specialized body parts, such as the extra set of jaws in a moray eel's throat. Other animals employ unique behaviors. A burrowing owl, for example, lures burying beetles closer by placing bits of the beetles' main food—cow droppings—near the entrances to their burrows!

I love animals and natural history, so it was fascinating to research these predators, their important roles in nature, and efforts to conserve, or save, these amazing creatures so we'll always have them in our world. I hope you'll enjoy reading about them just as much as I enjoyed writing about them!

—CHRISTINA WILSDON

I DIDN'T WATCH MUCH TELEVISION AS A KID GROWING UP IN SOUTH CAROLINA, spending my time instead running around outside. The shows I did view were almost always nature documentaries, especially about predators. I just couldn't get enough of the intensity of the chase, during which predators strive for dinner while prey run for their lives!

Not much has changed since then for me, for I am now an associate professor of wildlife science at the University of Washington, in Seattle, where I run the Predator Ecology Lab. My graduate students and I study the effects predators have on their ecosystems by killing and eating their prey—and, in some cases, by making their prey more cautious. We work with a lot of different species, from smaller predators like Canada lynx and coyotes all the way up to larger species like gray wolves, brown bears, and tiger sharks. Getting to learn about these majestic animals has been a tremendous privilege for me for two reasons. First, my job has allowed me to live out a childhood dream. (Indeed, as a reminder of my long-held desire to make a career of studying predators, my office is adorned by two drawings— both of killer whales chasing prey—that I completed as a fifth grader!) Second, many predators species are declining worldwide, so I enjoy sharing what I find out to help efforts to protect and recover them.

While reviewing *Ultimate Predatorpedia*, I found myself engrossed by the diversity of predators and the spectacular array of tactics they use to catch prey. I have discovered a lot about these captivating creatures in my twenty years as a researcher, but this book also reminded me how much remains to be discovered. I hope that, as you read through this wonderful encyclopedia, you'll be as inspired as I am to get out there and unravel the thrilling world of predators!

—AARON J. WIRSING, PH.D.

DISCOVERING PREDATORS

An African lion leaps on an African buffalo, which is not easy prey, even for this big cat.

WHAT IS A
PREDATOR?

What animals do you think of when you hear the word "predator"? Lions, tigers, and bears, perhaps. Wolves and sharks, too.

You probably *don't* think of robins or ladybugs. But these animals are predators as well. A predator is an animal that kills and eats other animals. For a lion, that means killing and eating other big animals, such as zebras. For a robin, that means pulling worms out of the soil. For a ladybug, it means eating aphids and other small insects.

Predators have bodies and behaviors that make them able to hunt, kill, and consume prey. These features have come into being by the process of evolution, or genetic change over time. These changes, or adaptations, help animals survive.

Some predators focus on just one kind of prey. Other predators eat a wide variety of other animals. Many predators can also snack on fruits and other plant parts. Predators also range widely from big to little—from enormous, jet-size blue whales to tiny mites smaller than a grain of sand.

BLUE WHALE
Balaenoptera musculus

The blue whale is the world's largest living animal. It's also the largest predator—but it feeds on extremely small prey. The blue whale eats small, shrimplike animals called krill. Krill are typically only about two inches (5 cm) long. The blue whale filters them out of the water using its giant mouth, which is full of long, shaggy strips called baleen. It can eat up to 40 million krill in one day.

COMMON FANGTOOTH
Anoplogaster cornuta

Yikes! This predatory fish looks like a sea monster, but it's actually only about six inches (15 cm) long. Its lower fangs are so large, it has special sockets in its head into which the teeth slide when it shuts its mouth. The fangtooth lives deep in the ocean, where it hunts fish and shrimps. It can eat a fish that is one-third the size of its own body.

ORNATE HAWK-EAGLE
Spizaetus ornatus

The ornate hawk-eagle of Central and South America mainly hunts and eats other birds. It zooms through the rain forest as it seeks birds both in the trees and on the forest floor. It's able to catch and kill birds that are bigger than it is.

BOBCAT
Lynx rufus

The bobcat is a cat, or feline, predator with big paws and a short tail. It preys mostly on small animals such as birds and rabbits, but it's also powerful enough to hunt deer. It kills small prey with a bite to the head or neck. It kills bigger animals by clamping its jaws on the prey's throat to suffocate it.

EYELASH PALM PIT VIPER
Bothriechis schlegelii

The eyelash palm pit viper hangs from trees by its tail when it lunges at prey to deliver a bite. Its fangs, which are usually folded back in its mouth, spring forward and stab into the bird, frog, or other animal serving as its target. The fangs inject a deadly fluid, called venom, to kill the prey.

PREDATORY MITE
Phytoseiulus persimilis

This mite is known by its scientific name, *Phytoseiulus persimilis*. It's only about .02 inch (0.5 mm) long—you need a hand lens to get a good look at it. But in the world of mites, it's a ferocious beast! It gobbles up other mites called spider mites and their eggs, too.

MEET THE
MEAT-EATERS

Here's a riddle for you: A carnivore is a meat-eater. Meat comes from animals. Predators eat animals. But not all predators are carnivores, even though they all eat meat.

When most people use the word "carnivore" they are simply using the word to mean anything that eats meat. But when you are talking about animals in a scientific way, "carnivore" has a specific meaning. It refers to a special order, or group, of animals. This group is called Carnivora.

The order Carnivora includes animals such as cats (from house cats to lions), wolves, and bears, as well as raccoons, weasels, skunks, otters, mongooses, hyenas, seals, and sea lions. That may seem like a strange grouping, but they all have something in common: their teeth.

Carnivores have special teeth called carnassial teeth. Carnassials are pairs of teeth in the sides of an animal's upper and lower jaw that move past each other like a pair of scissors. In most carnivores' mouths, these teeth slice meat like knives. When you see a cat or dog chewing on something with the side of its mouth, often with its head tilted, you know it's using its carnassials. Carnivores can only move their jaws up and down—not side to side the way you can to grind your food.

Over time, some carnivores' carnassials have adapted to eat other non-meat foods. Bears, for example, have carnassials that are good at crunching up plants.

But the predators that aren't in the order Carnivora don't go hungry! Birds, fish, invertebrates, and insect-eaters such as aardvarks all prey on other animals just fine without being carnivores.

DOG
Canis familiaris

TIGER
Panthera tigris

The European hedgehog eats some plants, but it mainly preys on insects. It also eats any other animal it can catch, such as snails, lizards, and small rodents. It's part of a group of animals known as insectivores—"insect-eaters."

One look at these teeth, and you know you're looking at a carnivore. Like other carnivores, a tiger has fangs. Fangs are enlarged canine teeth. People have canine teeth, too, but they're not enlarged like a carnivore's are. A tiger needs big canines for killing prey such as deer.

A dog chewing on a bone shows how a carnivore uses its carnassial teeth to slice and dice its food.

EUROPEAN HEDGEHOG
Erinaceus europaeus

Birds don't have teeth, but many of them are meat-eaters. This common merganser eats fish. The toothlike points on its bill work like teeth to help it grip its slippery prey.

COMMON MERGANSER
Mergus merganser

PREDATOR TOOLS

Hey hey, aye-aye! This animal lives on the island of Madagascar. It uses extra-long middle digits (fingers) on each hand to tap on a tree and then listens to hear if insect larvae are moving inside it, just beneath the bark. If so, it chews a hole in the bark and uses those same long fingers to pick out the grubs.

Predatory animals have many adaptations that help them catch and consume their prey. Some of these adaptations are easy to see, such as a lion's fangs, an eagle's talons, and a shark's jagged teeth.

Other adaptations are internal ones. For example, wolves, lions, and many other predators don't have collarbones like yours. (Your collarbones connect your shoulder blades to the breastbone in the middle of your chest.) These carnivores lack this link, but it allows them to be more flexible, to run faster, and to jump on prey without any danger of breaking that bone.

In addition, some adaptations are behaviors. Some behaviors involve motion, such as digging up prey, running after it, or quietly and slowly following or "stalking" it before giving chase. Other behaviors involve sitting still in a hiding spot and waiting for prey to come by. This is called sit-and-wait or "ambush" predation.

Some animals, such as spiders, set traps to catch prey. Others use tricks to lure prey closer. The more you read about predators, the more you'll find the same behaviors used again and again by a wide variety of animals.

Here are just a few of the amazing adaptations that help predators snag their prey.

PANTHER CHAMELEON
Furcifer pardalis

Zot! A chameleon hunts by creeping along a branch. It swivels its eyes around to look for an insect. When it spots one, both eyes snap forward to lock on the target. Its tongue shoots out and grabs the prey with its sticky tip.

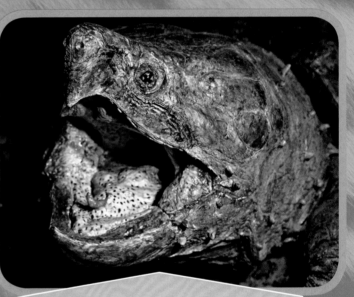

ALLIGATOR SNAPPING TURTLE
Macrochelys temminckii

Some animals trick other animals into coming closer so they can catch them. The alligator snapping turtle, for example, has a wormlike bit of flesh on its tongue that it wiggles to attract fish. Any hungry fish that swims up to check out the "worm" quickly becomes the turtle's lunch.

NET-CASTING SPIDER
Deinopis longipes

A net-casting spider hunts at night. It makes a little net—a mat-like web about the size of a stamp that is suspended between its front legs. It uses dabs of its own white poop to make marks on the ground or on a leaf below the net. This may help it aim at its target. Then it sits and waits for an insect to pass by so it can drop down, stretch open the net, and snare its prey.

FOOD WEBS

A pride of lions chase and pounce on a zebra. They pull it to the ground, kill it, and settle around its carcass to eat. When they're done, the lions will sleep for hours as they digest their huge meal. While they nap, other animals—vultures, hyenas, insects, and more—come to eat what's left of the carcass. Not a scrap will go to waste.

It's hard not to feel sorry for the zebra, but lions have to eat, too. A lion can't live by eating grass and other plants as a zebra can. Plants, zebras, and lions are all connected, like links in a chain. This chain even has a name: It's called a food chain.

A food chain starts with a living thing that can make food using energy from sunlight or chemicals. This kind of living thing is called a primary producer. In the lion-zebra-grass food chain, the grass is the primary producer. It uses energy from the sun to turn water and carbon dioxide from the air into food. The grass grows taller and makes seeds.

When the zebra eats the grass, the grass's energy and nutrients become part of the zebra. It provides the energy for the zebra to live, move, and grow. When the lion eats the zebra, all that energy and nutrition is on its way to becoming part of the lion.

What about those hyenas, vultures, and insects? They're parts of food chains, too. Add up all the food chains in a habitat, and you've got a food web. Food webs include many food chains as well as bacteria and other microscopic living things that break down dead plants and animals.

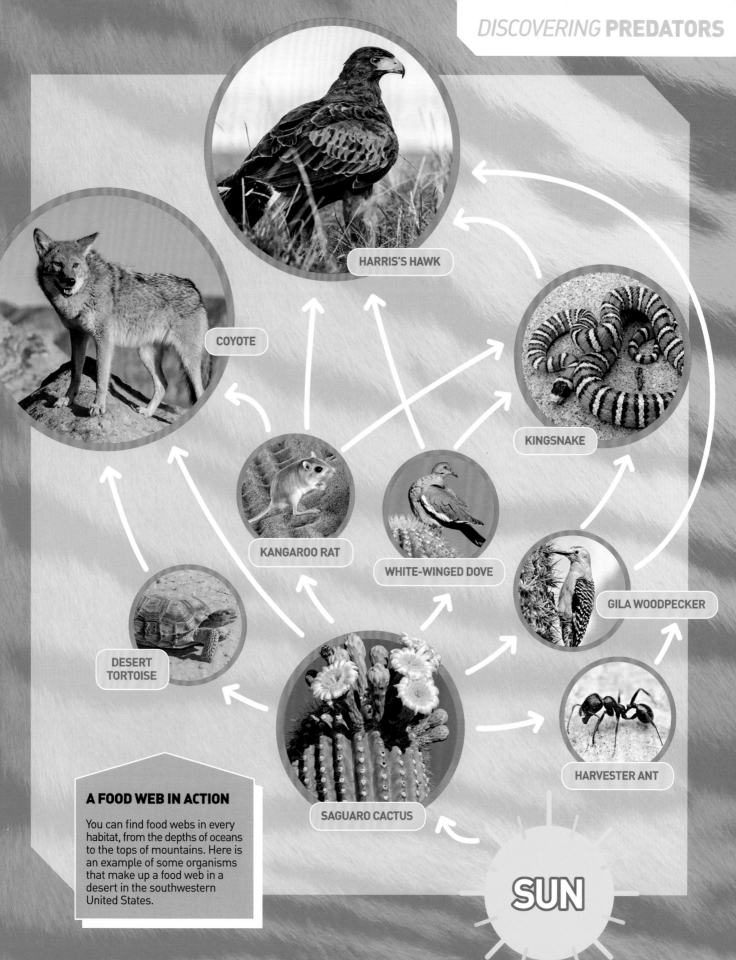

HARRIS'S HAWK

COYOTE

KINGSNAKE

KANGAROO RAT

WHITE-WINGED DOVE

GILA WOODPECKER

DESERT
TORTOISE

HARVESTER ANT

SAGUARO CACTUS

SUN

A FOOD WEB IN ACTION

You can find food webs in every habitat, from the depths of oceans to the tops of mountains. Here is an example of some organisms that make up a food web in a desert in the southwestern United States.

"THANKS, PREDATORS!"

Predators eat plants—sort of. They eat a lot of animals that are plant-eaters. Plant-eating animals are called herbivores. ("Herb" refers to plants.) Herbivores turn plant energy into energy for themselves. Predators get that energy by eating herbivores.

Some predators need to get all their energy by eating meat. Cats fall in this category. Other predators can get energy from plant foods as well as meat. Foxes, bears, and dogs belong to this group of predators that are called omnivores. ("Omni" means "all.")

So predators get energy from plants and plantlike organisms even if they don't eat them directly. But though predators don't eat plants, they still affect how plants grow and what kinds of plants grow in a habitat. Predators may seem like enemies of herbivores, but they can actually help keep habitats healthy for their prey.

In the United States, for example, gray wolves were almost completely wiped out in the lower 48 states by the mid-1900s. Ranchers and farmers saw wolves as killers of their sheep, cattle, and other animals. Hunters saw wolves as competitors for deer and other prey that they wanted to hunt themselves. This destruction of wolves and other predators was carried out with the support of the government, which likewise held the view that wolves were useless and a menace. Without wolf predators, however, deer populations grew very large in some places. All those deer ate a lot of plants. Deer sometimes starved to death in winter because there were too many deer and not enough plant food to sustain them all.

In Yellowstone National Park, wolves had been killed off by 1926. Starting in 1995, however, scientists began releasing wolves back into the park. Soon elk in the park were aware that their wolf predators had returned. The elk changed their behavior. They didn't spend as much time in one spot eating all the young trees growing there. Elk numbers also dropped as wolves preyed on them.

As a result, willows and other trees popped up in places they hadn't been for decades. More songbird species could live in this habitat because the trees were growing again. Beavers, which eat trees such as willows and use them to build dams and lodges, returned to these areas, too. That's a pretty big effect to have on the world just by hunting your dinner!

SEA OTTER
Enhydra lutris

TIGER SHARK
Galeocerdo cuvier

How might sharks help coral reefs stay healthy? Some sharks eat smaller predatory fish, which keeps their numbers in check. This removal of smaller predators might result in boosting the numbers of algae-eating fish. If algae covers a reef, it can smother coral animals, but algae-eating fish keep it under control.

Kelp forests are important habitats for young fish and other sea animals. Some animals, such as sea urchins, eat kelp. If sea urchin populations grow too large, kelp forests are harmed. The urchins not only eat the kelp but also break its hold on the seafloor. But sea otters love to eat sea urchins. By eating urchins, sea otters control their numbers and keep kelp forests healthy.

YELLOWSTONE WOLF

THE CLEANUP CREW

Pow! **A polar bear leaps as a seal pops its head up through a hole in the ice.** It drags the seal out of the water. The bear eats heartily, but it only devours the fat from the carcass. Fat is packed with energy, so it's the best part of a seal for a bear.

But the rest of the seal won't go to waste. Lots of animals will gobble up what's left. When an animal eats a dead animal that it didn't hunt and kill, it is said to be "scavenging." Little white arctic foxes, ravens, and younger polar bears are happy to scavenge seal carcasses.

Scavenging is a very common animal behavior because it's a great way to get a meal. Many predators are also scavengers. Polar bears, for example, scavenge whale carcasses. Arctic foxes follow polar bears to scavenge remains, but they mainly hunt lemmings and other rodents. Ravens eat just about anything. They are omnivores that will scavenge dead animals, prey on insects and mice, and dine on berries and seeds.

When scavengers are done noshing, it's time for tiny organisms such as bacteria and fungi to get to work. These organisms break down, or decompose, carrion into the very chemicals that formed the living animal. These chemicals go back into the soil, where they can be used again by plants and then animals. It's nature's own recycling system.

POLAR BEARS
Ursus maritimus

Two polar bears gobble up a ringed seal while seabirds prowl around them, waiting to snap up scraps.

AMPHIPOD
Iphimedia obesa

The ocean is home to scavengers just as the land is. This little animal is a species of amphipod. Amphipods feed on decaying bits of algae, plants, and animals. Big ocean animals such as sharks scavenge, too.

BLOWFLY
Lucilia sp.

Many insects also eat carrion (the remains of a dead animal). Blowflies lay their eggs in carrion so that their young will have a meal to eat when they hatch.

Some animals, such as vultures, feed mainly by scavenging. A turkey vulture, for example, can sniff out a dead animal from far away. It is able to feed on really rotten carcasses without getting sick from germs.

TURKEY VULTURE
Cathartes aura

WHEN PREDATORS MEET
EACH OTHER

Predators are not usually thrilled to meet up with other predators. Wolves, for example, form packs and cooperate with each other to hunt prey such as moose. But they don't want to join forces with other packs of wolves. Other wolves are competitors for food, and there is only so much food to go around.

So a wolf pack defends an area of land called its territory. The wolves howl and mark the edges of their territory with scents to tell other wolves, "Keep out! No trespassing!" Wolves don't want other species of predators hunting on their territory. They will kill any coyotes or foxes they find.

This behavior is called intraguild predation. It means, basically, predators hunting predators. A "guild" in the animal world means a group of living things that use the same resources. A wolf and a coyote are in the same predator guild, because they're both going after pretty much the same kinds of prey. Many predators will also kill the young of other predators. (And some predators, such as polar bears, eat other predators, such as seals.)

Scientists have found this kind of behavior in many mammal species—not just in the dog and cat families, but also among otters, minks, hyenas, and bears. Predatory birds, such as owls and hawks, are known to kill other predatory birds. Even scorpions and some species of beetles go after competing predators.

But the natural world is full of surprises. Scientists have also found a handful of predators that hunt with other species—including humans. Here are a few we know about.

Moray eels hunt at night by poking into crevices in a coral reef. Coral groupers are fish that hunt by day. But sometimes, the grouper and eel hunt as a team. The grouper shakes its head to tell the eel that there is prey in a narrow crevice that the grouper can't get into. Then it leads the eel to the crevice. The eel chases out the prey, which may be eaten by either the grouper or the eel.

In parts of Africa, a bird called the greater honeyguide hunts with humans. People call the bird with a whistle or sound that the bird recognizes as a hunting signal. It leads the people to a bee's nest. The humans open the nest to take the honey, and the honeyguide dives in to eat larvae and beeswax.

Sometimes, a coyote and a badger appear to hang out together while hunting. The badger digs to catch ground squirrels in their burrows, or underground dens. If the squirrel dashes out of its burrow to escape the badger, the coyote may catch it. If a squirrel dives into a den to escape a speedy coyote, that gives the badger a chance to catch it in the den. The two predators don't share the prey they catch, though.

CAN'T CATCH ME!

Predators are adapted to catch other animals—but prey animals are adapted to avoid getting caught. These animals are good at finding ways to live another day and not end up in a predator's stomach.

"Run for your life!" is the rule for many prey animals. Rabbits, deer, zebras, wildebeests, and gazelles are some of the many animals that race away from predators. Birds streak across the sky to get away from fast-flying falcons called merlins. Moths zigzag to escape bats.

Many prey animals hide from predators. A coral reef is filled with nooks and crannies where fish and other prey can hide. Crabs crawl under rocks in tide pools. Mice and other animals that live underground dive into burrows.

Freezing in place, on the other hand, is a way of hiding in plain sight. Many predators are quick to spot motion, but they lose track of their prey if it stops moving. A rabbit, for example, sits still as a stone for as long as it can to avoid being noticed.

Other prey animals, such as wildebeests, form large groups to foil predators. A group of animals has more eyes, ears, and noses on alert for danger, so a predator may be detected before it has a chance to make a surprise attack. It's also harder for a predator to pick out one target from a big group as individual animals move around. In addition, any single animal benefits from "hiding in the crowd."

Yet when predators manage to catch prey animals, the prey still have a chance. Many of them fight back with horns, hooves, teeth, or whatever they've got to escape. They also make use of armor, foul smells, vile-tasting substances, and even poison to keep predators from eating them. Many species have colors and shapes that cause them to blend in with their surroundings. This blending in is called camouflage.

THORNY DEVIL
Moloch horridus

The thorny devil is an Australian lizard that's a bag of self-defense tricks. Its tough skin is covered with thick, sharp spines. Its colors camouflage it in sand. It even moves in a lurching way that doesn't trigger a predator's sense of motion. If threatened, the thorny devil tucks its head between its front legs and presents a spiny bump to its attacker. It can also puff itself up so that it becomes a bigger and more difficult mouthful for a predator to handle.

VIRGINIA OPOSSUM
Didelphis virginiana

GIANT MALAYSIAN LEAF INSECT
Phyllium giganteum

Some animals play dead to avoid *becoming* dead. For example, a cornered opossum first tries to scare off a predator by hissing, drooling, and opening its mouth wide. But if it's attacked, it "drops dead." It falls over sideways with its tongue hanging out and eyes half shut. Even a bite won't make it move. Many predators won't eat food they didn't kill themselves, so the opossum's death act may save its life.

Predators may leave the Malaysian leaf insect alone simply because they can't find it. Its body and legs are shaped and colored like leaves, right down to details such as the ribbing that runs through a leaf. It even has patches of brown that look like the dead spots and damaged bits on a real leaf.

LUBBER GRASSHOPPER
Romalea microptera

The eastern lubber grasshopper of North America sports bright colors that warn predators to leave it alone because its body contains poisonous chemicals. It will also hiss, spit, and produce a foul-smelling foam if it's attacked.

PREDATORS OF
THE PAST

Plant-eating animals were munching on leaves and stems hundreds of millions of years ago—and there were plenty of predators around to munch on them.

The most famous of these ancient predators are meat-eating dinosaurs. These land-based predators included *Albertosaurus,* which hunted in packs like wolves, and *Deinosuchus,* which slashed with special killer claws measuring more than five inches (13 cm) long. The ancient seas also swarmed with predators such as *Tylosaurus,* a giant marine reptile with teeth not only in its jaws but also in the roof of its mouth. Flying reptiles flapped and soared across the sky.

When a massive asteroid struck Earth about 66 million years ago, it led to the extinction of many species, including dinosaurs (except for the ones that evolved to become today's birds). Since that time, other species have come and gone, including predators. Some predators disappeared in just the past 10,000 or so years, which is a blink of an eye in the history of Earth.

We know about dinosaurs and other long-gone animals because we've found bones, teeth, and other remains of them in rocks. These preserved remains are called fossils. A dinosaur bone, for example, might get covered with mud and sand. Over time, the mud and sand turn into stone. Meanwhile, some material in the bone is slowly replaced by minerals and turns into rock. By discovering these bones and putting them together, researchers can study them to find out what the animals looked like, what they ate, and how they lived.

MEGALODON SHARK

What does a shark the size of a subway car eat? Anything it wants! Megalodon was about one and a half times as long as the whale shark, the largest fish living today. It preyed on dolphins, whales, seals, and sea turtles. A fossil tooth from this shark is big enough to fill the palm of an adult's hand. Megalodon became extinct about 2.6 million years ago.

TITANOBOA

Scientists have found fossilized parts of the backbone of *Titanoboa,* a snake that died out about 56 million years ago. Based on the size of these bones, they estimate that *Titanoboa* was about 42.7 feet (13 m) long—the largest snake known. It's thought that it preyed on fish, turtles, and crocodiles.

SMILODON

Saber-toothed cats, known to scientists as *Smilodon,* lived from 2.5 million to 13,000 years ago. These lion-size predators once roamed North, South, and Central America. A *Smilodon* could open its mouth about twice as wide as one of today's big cats, and its fangs were almost seven inches (18 cm) long. These fangs were probably used to deliver a deep, stabbing bite to the throat of its prey.

TYRANNOSAURUS REX

Mighty *Tyrannosaurus rex* terrorized its prey for around 2 million years until it died out, or became extinct, about 66 million years ago. It chased its victims and also scavenged carrion. A *T. rex* was about 40 feet (12 m) long and up to 20 feet (6 m) tall, with jagged teeth the size of bananas. It ripped flesh off its prey with these teeth and then tossed back its head so the food fell into the back of its mouth. It's thought that *T. rex* could gulp down as much as 500 pounds (230 kg) of meat in just one bite.

GIANT PREHISTORIC DRAGONFLY

Dragonflies bigger than chickens zipped around about 300 million years ago. The insects' wings could span as much as 25 inches (65 cm), making it as wide as the wingspan of some modern hawks. Scientists are debating ideas about how changing oxygen levels in the air could be related to how big these dragonflies were.

RUNNERS, HOPPERS & LEAPERS

From the smallest island to the largest continent, predators can be found searching for their next meal. On a tiny island, the only predators you might see are insects—the birds and small animals inhabiting it might not have to worry about big predators, such as cats or foxes, if they're lucky. But you'll find predators from alligators to zorillas on bigger land areas.

Legs come in handy if you're a land predator. You can't run, leap, grab, or claw without them! Leggy land predators may have as few as two legs (hello, birds!) or more than 350 in the case of some centipedes. However, you don't need legs to be a land predator. Snakes do just fine without them. Here are a few of the many animals that hunt on land.

FISHER
Pekania pennanti

What does a fisher eat? Not fish, that's for sure! The fisher hunts rabbits, hares, rodents, and birds. It's also one of the few predators that tackles the prickly porcupine. It attacks a porcupine by scampering in circles around it, waiting for a chance to strike its face, which has no quills. After killing the porcupine, the fisher flips it over to expose its belly, which also lacks quills. Fishers live in North America.

AMUR LEOPARD
Panthera pardus orientalis

Many leopards prowl the hot grasslands of Africa, but the Amur leopard's home is in eastern Russia. Unlike its southern cousin, it knows all about snow because winter is very cold and snowy where it lives. It grows a long winter coat to keep warm. This rare and highly endangered species mainly hunts deer, hares, and wild pigs.

ROADRUNNER
Geococcyx californianus

Roadrunners can fly, but they'd rather run. They could beat you in a footrace! This bird hunts small animals such as rodents, lizards, and scorpions. It can even kill a rattlesnake by pecking its head over and over again. Sometimes it may team up with another roadrunner to do the job, with one bird flapping around to distract the snake while the other attacks. Roadrunners live in the southwestern United States, Mexico, and parts of Central America.

GOLDEN GROUND BEETLE
Carabus auratus

In the dark of night, a golden ground beetle sets out to hunt worms, insects, slugs, and snails. It catches its prey with its huge jaws, called mandibles. This beetle is a European species that was released in North America in the 1940s to help control a garden pest called the gypsy moth.

DHOLE
Cuon alpinus

The dhole is a wild dog, or canid, found in parts of Asia. It hunts in packs to catch deer, wild pigs, and other hoofed animals. A dhole on its own catches rabbits and small prey. Instead of barking, dholes make an odd whistling sound. This endangered predator shares its range with tigers, bears, wolves, leopards, and snow leopards.

29

WADERS, SWIMMERS & FLOATERS

Predators swim, scuttle, and float in all the watery places on Earth.
Lakes, ponds, and rivers are home to a wide range of predators such as frogs, catfish, and diving ducks that eat fish. Sharks and other predatory fish prowl the oceans. Even a puddle in your neighborhood may contain a mighty, microscopic tardigrade, or "water bear." Carnivorous tardigrades eat smaller tardigrades.

Some of these predators, such as polar bears, river otters, and seals, split their time between land and water. Many live their entire lives in water. All of them have adaptations that help them swim, dive, and survive in water.

Here are a few of the many animals that hunt in water.

BOTTLENOSE DOLPHIN
Tursiops truncatus

A bottlenose dolphin's grinning jaws are lined with sharp, cone-shaped teeth. They're perfect for seizing fish, squid, and other seafood. But first it must find its prey. A dolphin does this by using sound. It makes clicking noises that bounce off objects and send echoes back to the dolphin's ears. The echoes tell the dolphin where the prey is and even how big it is. This behavior is called echolocation.

GREAT HAMMERHEAD SHARK
Sphyrna mokarran

The great hammerhead shark's oddly shaped head helps it find prey in the ocean. Its sensory organs are dotted across its wide head. These organs detect the small amount of electricity given off by animals' bodies and help it find stingrays hiding in sand. The wide head is also used to hold rays down while the shark bites the ray's fins. Hammerheads also eat other kinds of fish, as well as animals such as squid, octopuses, and crabs.

PEACOCK MANTIS SHRIMP
Odontodactylus scyllarus

The peacock mantis shrimp lives in warm waters near and on reefs in the Indian and Pacific Oceans. It kills prey such as crabs, snails, and even fish with a punch of its special hammerlike claws. These claws can smack at a speed of 75 feet a second (23 m/s). You'd miss the movement if you blinked! The punch is strong enough to smash glass.

BAIKAL SEAL
Pusa sibirica

Most seals hunt in the salty waters of oceans and seas. But the Baikal seal is found only in the freshwater of Lake Baikal in Russia and nearby rivers. At night, Baikal seals feast on Baikal oilfish, which are also only found in this lake. While hunting, Baikal seals can stay underwater for 25 minutes or more without coming up for air.

WHITE STURGEON
Acipenser transmontanus

The white sturgeon is the largest freshwater fish in North America. It can grow to be 20 feet (6 m) long, but most are half that size. It hunts fish, worms, and other prey in deep, murky water at the bottom of rivers. It finds prey with the help of stringlike barbels hanging from its snout that can sense smells. Its taste buds are also on the outside of its toothless mouth. When it finds prey, it slurps it up like a vacuum cleaner.

SOARING, FLAPPING & DIVING

Predators that can fly often pluck their prey from the ground or the water. Think of a hawk snatching a rabbit off the ground in its talons, or an eagle grabbing a fish out of the sea. Some predators, such as brown pelicans and seabirds called gannets, fly high and then plunge from the sky to dive deep in water to catch fish.

But some flying predators catch their prey while in flight. They may even eat as they fly! These predators are adapted in different ways to go after flying prey and catch it while they're both in the air.

Here are a few of the many animals that hunt in the sky.

SPECTRAL BAT
Vampyrum spectrum

Most bats eat insects. Some bats eat fruit and nectar. A few sip blood. But there are also some bats that feast on fish, reptiles, small mammals, and birds. The spectral bat of Central and northern South America is one of these flying carnivores. It hunts by flying low to the ground and then pouncing. It is thought that the bat uses its sense of smell to find birds that have a strong scent.

BEARDED ROBBER FLY
Efferia pogonias

Robber flies have big eyes for spotting prey and long, bristly legs for catching it. They mainly hunt insects, and some species focus on certain prey, such as bees. Many robber flies hunt like hawks—they sit on a high perch, watch for their meal, and then fly off to pounce on it. The bearded robber fly can chase and catch flies in midair. It injects its deadly saliva into its prey and takes it to its perch to eat.

BAT HAWK
Macheiramphus alcinus

The bat hawk's name is a clue to what it eats! Bats form a large part of the bat hawk's meals. A bat hawk also eats other fast-flying birds such as swifts and swallows. It chases down its prey at high speed and catches it with its feet. Then the captured bat or bird is swallowed whole as the hawk keeps flying to find more prey. Bat hawks hunt mainly at dawn and dusk.

MERLIN
Falco columbarius

The merlin is a speedy bird of prey that hunts mainly small to medium-size birds. Its fast flapping lets it zip at speeds up to 30 miles an hour (48 km/h) and even faster when it chases prey. A merlin zooms at its prey from the side or may swoop up at it from below. The high-speed chase continues until the prey is exhausted. Then the merlin grabs it. Merlins also snatch dragonflies from the air.

COMMON SWIFT
Apus apus

The common swift swoops through the air, eating insects as it goes. It can open its little beak very wide to scoop up its flying food. They may fly more than a mile (1.6 km) high to catch bugs. Common swifts spend up to 10 months of the year in the air! They are able to glide for long distances, and that's probably when they get a chance to nap. They land only to nest and raise young in the breeding season.

PREDATORS
AND US

Humans have had a relationship with predatory animals for a long time. Prehistoric cave paintings in parts of Europe, for example, show powerful cave bears, which probably both inspired and terrified prehistoric people. Lions have appeared as symbols of strength and bravery in stories and art throughout history. Today, sports teams around the world are named after predators such as bears, panthers, lions, and eagles.

But people have also looked at predators as enemies in different places at different times. Predators sometimes kill domestic animals such as cattle, sheep, and chickens. Some people also dislike that predators hunt deer, fish, and other animals that they want for themselves.

Today, we know that predators are an important part of a healthy ecosystem—the community of living things interacting with each other and the nonliving parts of a habitat. People around the world are finding ways of living with predators while keeping themselves—and their livestock—safe. Here are just a few of those stories.

People have used big, strong dogs to guard their animals for thousands of years. This practice died out in many places as the numbers of wolves, bears, and other predators grew smaller over time. In the past few decades, however, guard dogs have come back on the job.

In the western United States, for example, dogs protect some flocks of sheep from predators such as coyotes, cougars, bears, and even wolves. Ranchers are also trying out electric fencing and flapping strips of plastic called fladry to scare predators away.

In parts of Asia, herders were upset that snow leopards sometimes killed their sheep and goats. Snow leopards, which are threatened, were being shot as a result. In an effort to help both herders and snow leopards, a special project was started in 1998 that gets herders to buy insurance for their sheep and goats. The herder pays a small fee—the insurance cost—and if a snow leopard kills a goat or sheep, the herder gets paid the full price of the animal. Herders are also learning to build better fences and new ways of preventing snow leopards from hunting their herd.

In Kenya and other parts of East Africa, lions hunting at night sometimes kill cattle. The loss of cattle is very hard on herders, and they often respond by killing lions—the most obvious targets. Without lions around, however, olive baboons increase in number. These animals then raid farm fields and eat crops. Kids sometimes have to miss school to stay home and help protect crops from baboons.

But now some herders are protecting their animals by putting them in a special corral at night. This corral is called a "living wall." The wall is a blend of two kinds of fences. One is the *boma*, a traditional African fence made of thorny plants. The other is a modern chain-link fence. Live trees form the fence posts. The living walls are nearly 100 percent predator-proof.

PROTECTING PREDATORS

With its sharp teeth and claws, a tiger doesn't look like an animal that needs help. But the tiger is one of many endangered species—animals that may become extinct if people don't make an effort to save them.

Protecting animals, plants, and other living things and their habitats is called conservation. To conserve things means not to waste them or ruin them. When we conserve habitats and living things, we make sure that they continue to function properly and that they'll exist in the future.

Many predators are protected by laws that limit or forbid hunting them or selling their body parts. However, one of the most important ways to help predators—and their prey—is to conserve their habitat. Protecting an ecosystem is vital for all the animals and other organisms that share it.

Here are a few examples of efforts that have helped predators survive.

PEREGRINE FALCON
Falco peregrinus

The peregrine falcon (pp. 130–131) is a fast-flying bird that preys on other birds. In 1964, it became extinct in the eastern United States. This was a result of the falcons eating birds that had eaten insects poisoned by a pesticide called DDT. The DDT made the falcons lay eggs with thin shells that cracked. DDT was banned in 1972 in the United States, but the peregrines were already gone. So a new program, the Peregrine Recovery Plan, got started in 1979. Peregrine chicks were hatched and raised in captivity. Later, they were set free. The program was a success. Today, peregrines once again zoom across the sky from coast to coast.

CHATHAM ISLAND TAIKO
Pterodroma magentae

The Chatham Island taiko is a seabird that breeds on only one island off the coast of New Zealand. It lays its eggs in burrows dug in forests and catches fish and squid at sea.

Long ago, people on the islands gathered taiko chicks as food. But the birds' habitat started changing in the mid-1800s. Farmers brought sheep, cattle, and pigs to the island. Rats and cats came with them. The grazing animals harmed the forests, while pigs, rats, and cats ate chicks. Today, fewer than 200 taikos exist.

Farmers stepped up to help save taikos in 1983 by donating land where the few remaining taikos nested. This area became the Tuku Nature Reserve. Rats and other predators are strictly controlled in the reserve, and sheep and cattle are kept out. In 2006, a predator-proof fence was built around an area beside the reserve. In 2014, chicks hatched in this special area for the first time.

GRIZZLY BEAR
Ursus arctos

Grizzly bears used to roam the mountains in central Washington in the United States. Today, there may be just a few—scientists do not have a firm head count for them, and sightings are rare. That may change because there are plans to reintroduce grizzly bears to their former home. One plan brings in grizzlies from Montana and Canada. These bears would wear radio collars so scientists can track them. The goal is to have 200 bears in these mountains within the next 100 years.

AMUR TIGER
Panthera tigris altaica

Fewer than 4,000 tigers exist in the wild. Poaching (illegal hunting) has driven these big cats to the edge of extinction. About 540 of those tigers are Amur tigers—a number that sounds terribly small. But for this tiger species, it is a sign of success.

Amur tigers used to live across parts of eastern Russia, northern China, and the Korean peninsula. By 1940, only about 40 Amur tigers remained in the wild after many years of hunting and habitat loss. Then Russia's government passed laws protecting tigers. China started conserving tiger habitats. Thanks to these efforts, the tigers' numbers grew.

By 2008, the species went from being considered "critically endangered" to "endangered" according to the IUCN (International Union for Conservation of Nature). This was a small but important step in the right direction. People are still working to continue protecting these big cats.

TOO HOT
TO HUNT?

Hotter summers and shorter winters in some places ... super-hurricanes in others ... warmer waters and melting ice. These changes and many others may be linked to a worldwide problem called climate change.

Climate is the kind of weather conditions that are normal for an area over the span of many years. Climate change is any large, long-lasting change in Earth's climate. Since 1880, Earth's average temperature has risen by as much as 1.8°F (1.0°C). About two-thirds of this rise has happened since 1975. That might not sound like a big increase, but keep in mind that a worldwide temperature *drop* in that amount would cause an ice age to happen!

What's the cause? Scientists point to an increase in heat-trapping greenhouse gases building up in the atmosphere. These gases are being created by the burning of fuels such as oil, coal, and natural gas. More greenhouse gases trapping heat means rising temperatures, warmer oceans, and climate change across the land.

Here are a few examples of how climate change might affect predatory animals.

CORAL REEFS: IN HOT WATER

Corals in tropical reefs are sensitive to changes in water temperature. If the water gets too warm, the tiny coral animals may eject the algae inside them. Algae make food for the corals, so by kicking out the algae, the coral may starve and die.

Without living coral reefs, many coral-feeding animals will lose both their prey and their home. Predators that feed on coral reef fish, shrimps, and other prey will also go hungry. The entire coral reef food web ends up in tatters.

POLAR BEARS: FEELING THE HEAT

The polar bear (pp. 72–73) is one of the best known examples of how an animal can be affected by climate change. Polar bears need sea ice so they can hunt seals. But as the climate warms, sea ice is melting sooner in spring and freezing later in fall in places such as Canada's Hudson Bay. This means the bears are stuck on land for longer spans of time with barely anything to eat. The early melting of ice in spring cuts down on how much time they have to hunt right when seal pups are being born.

BURROWING OWLS: FIRES AND FLOODS

The little burrowing owl lives in grasslands, deserts, and other wide-open spaces in parts of North, Central, and South America. It is most closely linked to the "towns" of prairie dogs—large areas filled with burrows—because it lives in old prairie dog burrows.

Like other owls, it catches prey with its feet. Its prey includes rodents, birds, small reptiles, and insects. It uses a clever trick to lure dung beetles within grabbing range: It lines part of its burrow with cow poop.

Burrowing owls are threatened, however, because people have poisoned prairie dogs and turned prairie dog towns into farmland. Now the owls face new threats due to climate change. Some burrowing owl habitats may suffer from water shortages and grassland fires. In other places, extra-heavy rain might flood their burrows.

FANGS, CLAWS & GAPING JAWS

A yawning jaguar reveals its sharp fangs, which are used to grip and kill prey.

ALL ABOUT PREDATORY MAMMALS

If you have a cat or a dog at home, you're living with a predatory mammal! A mammal is an animal that has hair and makes milk for its young. The mammal group includes animals ranging from little bumblebee bats, which are about the size of big bumblebees, to the mighty blue whale, which is longer than two school buses! (Yes, even whales have hair, at least at the beginning of their lives.)

Predatory mammals have body parts and abilities to help them catch prey. You can see some of these features, or adaptations, just by looking at a cat or a dog.

For example, a variety of predatory mammals have eyes that both face forward. This placement gives them vision that helps them judge how far away something is. That "something" is often the prey that the mammal is trying to catch. Animals that are hunted often have eyes set more on the sides of their heads, which helps them see all around them and watch out for predators.

A mammal may also have claws that are adapted for clutching or killing prey. Think of the sharp, curved claws of a cat!

Many predatory mammals have teeth that are adapted for use as tools for catching and eating prey. Some of these predators are called carnivores.

Most people use the word "carnivore" to mean "meat-eater." But scientists use it to describe animals that have long canine teeth (fangs) and a few back teeth, called carnassials, which are shaped so they work like scissor blades to slice through their prey's skin and meat. Carnivores can't move their jaws from side to side—only up and down.

CARACAL
Caracal caracal

The caracal is a wild cat found in parts of Africa, central and southwestern Asia, and India. It mostly eats small animals, such as mice and small antelopes, which it catches by chasing and then leaping on them. It can even leap 10 feet (3 m) to knock a bird out of the air! It's a carnivore, like all other cats. And like most cats, its claws stay tucked inside its paws and only pop out when they're needed. This helps keep the claws sharp.

BLACK BEAR
Ursus americanus

Who says a carnivore can't eat veggies? Many carnivores, such as bears, also eat fruit. Bears' back teeth, or molars, have changed over time to be flatter and more useful for crushing plant parts such as roots. A black bear actually eats far more plant food than meat. It devours nuts, roots, and leaves as well as berries and other fruits.

MANED WOLF
Chrysocyon brachyurus

The maned wolf is a long-legged, shaggy member of the dog group, which also includes animals such as foxes and coyotes. It lives in parts of South America. About half of a maned wolf's food is fruits and vegetables. It also eats rodents, rabbits, and insects. It hunts by tapping with one of its front paws to scare up prey from underground. Then it pounces on the animal as it tries to escape.

FISH-EATING BAT
Myotis vivesi

Some bat species eat fruits and flowers. Many bats prey on insects. But you can surely guess what the fish-eating bat eats! At night, this bat swoops down on ponds and streams to snatch fish from the water with its long legs, big feet, and claws. A fish-eating bat can catch 30 fish in just one night!

SEA OTTER
Enhydra lutris

Sea otters catch prey such as crabs, clams, and sea urchins underwater. A sea otter often eats its prey by floating on its back and using its chest as a dining table. Also on the "table" is a rock, which the otter manipulates to smash open clam shells. Otters even use rocks underwater to pry shellfish off surfaces.

WALRUS
Odobenus rosmarus

The blubbery walrus is a predator that swims quickly and gracefully underwater. That's where it hunts for shellfish such as clams to eat. This carnivore doesn't use its big tusks to eat them—it just sucks in the food like a vacuum! Some male walruses are known to prey on seabirds and seals.

43

A lioness chases a warthog on the grasslands of the Serengeti in Africa. A warthog sometimes escapes by running to a hole in the ground, backing into it, and then facing its predator with its sharp tusks ready for fighting back.

AFRICAN LION

The African lion is often called the "king of beasts." This mighty cat is respected around the world for its strength and power.

Lions are the only members of the cat family that live in big family groups. A group of lions is called a pride. A pride is made up of female lions, called lionesses, and their cubs, as well as a few males. A typical pride includes three to six lionesses and two or three males, plus cubs. The lionesses form the pride's base. They are all related to each other. The male lions may be brothers, but they may also just be buddies.

Lions hunt mainly at night and in the dim hours around sunrise and sunset. Most often, a hunt begins with a lion sneaking up on, or stalking, her prey. When the lion gets close, it suddenly rushes at its prey and attacks. Lions may split up, with one lion stalking and the others hiding in different places to attack the prey when it runs by.

A lion attacks by using its paws to hit its prey and knock it over, or by jumping on it to pull it down. Then it kills by biting the prey's throat or neck. If a large animal doesn't die from this bite, the lion can suffocate it with a bite that covers its nose and mouth.

Lionesses do most of the hunting, but the males aren't just lazy loafers. A male can kill his own prey, and he can help the pride take down bigger animals. Males also prowl the pride's territory and keep out unfamiliar males that would try to kill the cubs.

FACTS

FAMILY Felidae

OTHER COMMON NAMES Lion

SCIENTIFIC NAME *Panthera leo*

SIZE 5.2 to 8.2 feet (1.6 to 2.5 m), not including tail

FOOD Zebras, wildebeests, antelopes, and other large hoofed animals; also rodents, baboons, porcupines, and carrion

HABITAT Savannas, grasslands, woodlands

RANGE Sub-Saharan Africa; small population of a subspecies in Gir Forest of India

Lions roar to keep in touch with others in their pride. They also roar to tell unfamiliar lions to stay away or get out of their territory. A lion's roar can be heard five miles (8 km) away!

BENGAL TIGER

FACTS

FAMILY Felidae

OTHER COMMON NAMES
Indian tiger

SCIENTIFIC NAME
Panthera tigris tigris

SIZE 4.8 to 9.8 feet (1.5 to 3 m), not including tail

FOOD Large hoofed animals and smaller prey of various species

HABITAT Forests, grasslands

RANGE Bangladesh, India, Nepal, Bhutan

With its bright orange fur striped with black, you'd think the Bengal tiger would be as easy to see in the wild as an electric sign! But its bold markings are actually a form of camouflage. They help a tiger blend in with strips of sunlight and streaky shadows in forests and grasslands.

Bengal tigers hunt various kinds of deer and antelope, as well as wild boars and water buffalo. They also snack on smaller animals such as monkeys, foxes, hares, and birds.

A Bengal tiger typically hunts alone. A hungry tiger may wait near a water hole to ambush prey, or slowly stalk prey before making a fast lunge. It grabs large prey by the throat or snout to suffocate it. Smaller animals die from a bite to the neck or head.

Like lions, tigers will gladly gobble up the leftovers from other predators' meals. They will also drive other predators away to steal their kills. If the prey is a large hoofed animal, a tiger can feed on it for days and will hang around until nothing is left but scraps. A tiger can gulp down as much as 88 pounds (40 kg) of meat in one meal!

The Bengal tiger is one of five kinds of tigers alive in the wild today.

These big cats live alone most of the time. A female will pair up with a male for a while to mate. She gives birth to two or more cubs. The cubs stay with her for two or three years so they can learn to hunt and live on their own.

Tigers in the wild are at risk of extinction. The main threats they face are habitat loss and poaching.

A tiger usually hunts at night and may roam many miles to find food.

Tigers are excellent hunters, but they're not above stealing! They often swipe kills from leopards, jackals, and other predators.

Like other big cats, leopards also roar, but their roar isn't like a lion's bellow. It sounds more like rasps, grunts, and snores mixed up with the sound of a saw slicing through wood. This leopard is snarling a warning.

AFRICAN LEOPARD

It's not easy to "spot" a leopard! This big cat's spots are actually camouflage. The spots help it blend in with patches of light and dark on rocks and among plants. They also break up its shape in the eyes of its prey. It doesn't instantly look cat-shaped the way it would if it were a solid color.

Even though it has great camouflage, a leopard likes to hunt at night. If it's hunting in a habitat where it can hide in tall grass and shrubs, it can ambush prey—it will sit and wait to surprise an animal that comes near. If it's hunting in a more wide-open place, it will stalk its prey instead, creeping up quietly until it's very close and then suddenly springing at it. Leopards can also leap from trees onto their victims.

A leopard kills big animals by strangling them with a bite to the throat or by engulfing the snout with its jaws. Small prey is killed in one snap to the neck or head.

Like tigers, leopards hide their leftovers so they're not gobbled up by scavengers such as vultures or other predators. A leopard may tuck its prey into bushes, caves, or holes. Unlike tigers, leopards will even drag their prey up into trees! A leopard is so strong, it can grab and drag a deer up into the branches.

A mother leopard keeps her fuzzy cubs in a den when she's hunting. A den may be a rocky cave, a pocket of thick plants, or a similar shelter. She moves her cubs often to keep them safe from lions, hyenas, and other predators. Cubs drink milk until they're about three months old. They stay with their mom until they're almost two years old.

FACTS

FAMILY Felidae

OTHER COMMON NAMES Leopard

SCIENTIFIC NAME *Panthera pardus pardus*

SIZE 4.25 to 6.25 feet (1.3 to 1.9 m), not including tail

FOOD Medium-size and large hoofed animals, as well as smaller prey, such as reptiles, birds, and insects

HABITAT Rain forests, mountains, savannas; deserts and other dry lands

RANGE Sub-Saharan and northeastern Africa

The Amur leopard lives in forests of eastern Russia. It's the world's rarest big cat. Scientists estimate that fewer than 60 remain in an area called Land of the Leopard National Park.

A snow leopard can leap up to 30 feet (10 m) in one bound.

SNOW LEOPARD

Snow leopards are known as "the ghost of the mountains." They get this name because they're not often seen. They are rare, for one thing. In addition, their spotted coats camouflage them beautifully in their snowy, rocky home.

Snow leopards have other adaptations that help them survive in their cold environment, too. Their fur is very thick and fluffy. Even their paws are covered in thick fur. The paws are also wide, which helps a snow leopard walk on snow as if it were wearing snowshoes.

The snow leopard has the longest tail compared to its body size of any cat. Its tail can be as much as 41 inches (105 cm) long. Some snow leopards have tails that are long enough to stretch all the way to their necks!

But this amazing tail isn't just a decoration. It helps a snow leopard balance as it leaps and runs on steep, rocky slopes. This big cat also wraps its long tail around its body to keep warm.

One of the snow leopard's favorite prey species is the blue sheep, also known as a bharal. A bharal's blue-gray coat helps it hide in plain sight on rocky hillsides, but the sharp-eyed snow leopard can still find it. Snow leopards hunt mainly at dawn, dusk, and night, but also by day in remote areas.

Like other big cats, snow leopards may ambush prey or stalk it. A leopard tries to snag its prey with its claws or knock it down before seizing it. Then it hangs around the carcass for a few days, feasting on it down to the last scrap.

FACTS

FAMILY Felidae

OTHER COMMON NAMES Ounce

SCIENTIFIC NAME *Panthera uncia*

SIZE 3 to 3.8 feet (0.9 to 1.2 m), not including tail

FOOD Blue sheep (bharal), ibex, and other hoofed animals, as well as hares, marmots, and other small animals

HABITAT Cold, rocky mountains

RANGE Central Asia

Snow leopards are threatened due to poaching, habitat loss, and less prey to hunt because their prey are also scarce. Many people are working to protect these cats and their habitat.

A cheetah can cover 22 feet (6.7 m) in just one stride. That's almost three times as long as the stride of a top Olympic sprinter!

CHEETAH

***Zoom!* Meet the cheetah, the world's fastest land** animal. This speedy cat can zip from a standstill to 60 miles an hour (96 km/h) in just three seconds. Its amazing speed lets it catch other fast runners such as gazelles.

A cheetah's body is adapted for speed from nose to tail. Its nose has nostrils bigger than those of other cats to help it take bigger breaths. This helps give it the oxygen it needs to fuel its blazing speed. As it runs, its tail swings to help it make tight turns and keep its balance. Its spine is very flexible, which allows the cheetah to bend its body and take incredibly long strides. Even its claws help with speed. Unlike other cats, a cheetah can only partly pull in its claws. As a result, they stick out just enough to give the cheetah a great grip on the ground as it runs.

But a cheetah has to put in some work before it starts running. First it has to pick out its prey using its sharp eyesight. Cheetahs usually hunt by day. The dark marks that drip from the corners of their eyes may help stop bright sunlight from overpowering their vision.

Once the cheetah has selected its victim, it stalks it. The cheetah hunkers down on its long legs and slowly paces toward its prey. If the prey looks up, the cheetah freezes. It doesn't move until the prey goes back to grazing. Then, when the cheetah is close enough, it launches an attack. It catches its prey by snagging it with a claw or batting it to knock it down. It kills large prey by clamping its jaws on its throat until it suffocates. Smaller prey is dispatched with a bite to the neck.

Unfortunately, cheetahs can't outrun threats such as habitat loss and poaching. It's estimated that only 7,100 still live in the wild. Efforts to help save these animals include working with farmers to protect their cattle from cheetahs without killing them.

FACTS

FAMILY Felidae

OTHER COMMON NAMES Hunting leopard

SCIENTIFIC NAME *Acinonyx jubatus*

SIZE 3.5 to 4.5 feet (1.1 to 1.4 m), not including tail

FOOD Small antelopes, gazelles, hares

HABITAT Savannas, deserts

RANGE Sub-Saharan Africa, northern Iran

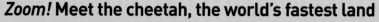

Some cheetahs have spots that blend together to form blotches and stripes. They're called king cheetahs, but they're the same species as cheetahs with regular spots. In house cats, this same kind of color pattern produces stripy orange-and-silver tabby cats.

JAGUAR

FACTS

FAMILY Felidae

OTHER COMMON NAMES None

SCIENTIFIC NAME
Panthera onca

SIZE 5 to 6 feet (1.5 to 1.8 m), not including tail

FOOD Medium-size mammals and reptiles, as well as small animals

HABITAT Rain forests, tropical forests, scrublands, wooded grasslands, mangrove forests, wetlands

RANGE Northern and central South America from northern Mexico to northern Argentina, possibly small population in southwestern United States

The jaguar is the world's third largest cat (tigers and lions take the top two spots).

Many people think cats don't like water, but the jaguar is definitely a feline that likes to swim. They often live near water and will readily swim across rivers. They even hunt in water to catch fish, turtles, and crocodile-like animals called caimans.

On land, jaguars pounce on animals such as deer, piglike animals called peccaries, and the South American tapir, a pony-size animal with a trunk-like snout. Jaguars also eat the world's largest rodent, the capybara (picture a supersize guinea pig). Oh, and giant anteaters, sloths, monkeys, and armadillos, too ... the jaguar's menu goes on and on!

A jaguar has a powerfully muscled, stocky body and stocky legs. It may wait in a tree for prey to pass by and then jump on it. Like other cats, it also stalks and chases prey. Jaguars are even known to float down rivers and leap out of the water to seize animals resting on shore.

The jaws of a jaguar are so strong, they can bite through a sea turtle's shell. A jaguar often kills even large prey by biting right through its skull or neck.

These cats were once heavily hunted and trapped so their spotted skins could be used for fancy fur coats. Thanks to laws that were passed beginning in the 1970s, hunting jaguars for their skins isn't a main threat to their survival anymore. But habitat loss is, because forests are being cut for lumber and to make way for ranches. Farmers and ranchers sometimes kill jaguars, too.

Scientists are working with people in the jaguar's range to plan a path, or "wildlife corridor," which will connect the many places where jaguars live. Jaguars and other animals could travel safely along this corridor across many countries to find food, shelter, and mates. Scientists are also helping ranchers find better ways to keep their animals safe from predators.

In 2011, a male jaguar was discovered roaming forests in Arizona, U.S.A. A contest was held to name the big cat. The winning name was El Jefe, which means "the boss" in Spanish.

A cougar can leap 30 feet (9 m) in one bound. It can also jump 15 feet (4.6 m) straight up to climb a cliff or get over a wall—that's higher than any other cat can jump.

COUGAR

If someone showed you a cougar cub, you'd probably think it was the young of a jaguar or a leopard. It's covered with spots. But by the time it's about nine months old, the cub will have lost its baby spots. The speckled coat is replaced by the solid tawny color of an adult cat.

Cougars are one of the most widespread mammals in the Western Hemisphere—the part of Earth that contains North, Central, and South America among other lands. That's true even though they've disappeared from much of their original range.

Cougars once roamed from coast to coast in the lower 48 part of the United States and in areas of Canada. By the early 1900s, however, they had been killed off in nearly all the eastern part of their range by farmers, ranchers, and government hunters. The only cougars remaining in the eastern United States are a small population of about two hundred in Florida, where they're known as Florida panthers. They live in swamplands in southern Florida.

A cougar hunts mainly at dawn, dusk, and night. It will walk up to 6.2 miles (10 km) a night to search for prey that it can stalk and then chase. It also lies in hiding to ambush animals. It knocks down its prey with its paws. Small prey are killed with a bite to the head or neck. A cougar can also kill a hoofed animal with a bite to the neck, but if the prey is very large, the cougar may deliver a strangling bite to its throat.

Then the cougar drags its prey away to feast. It may gobble up as much as 10 pounds (4.5 kg) of meat in one meal if it hasn't eaten for a while. After eating, it kicks leaves and grass over the carcass to hide it from scavengers. This behavior is called caching. It will come back to dine on the leftovers for a few days.

FACTS

FAMILY Felidae

OTHER COMMON NAMES
Mountain lion, puma, catamount, panther

SCIENTIFIC NAME
Puma concolor

SIZE 3.3 to 5.3 feet (1 to 1.6 m), not including tail

FOOD Deer, elk, and other medium to large hoofed mammals; small mammals and other small animals such as birds and reptiles

HABITAT Desert scrublands, wooded grasslands, woodlands, forests, swamps

RANGE Southwestern Canada, western United States, Central America, South America

The cougar has been given a lot of common names over time. You will often hear a cougar referred to as a puma or a mountain lion. European settlers called them tigers and panthers. Some people referred to them as red or deer tigers. An old name for the cougar is catamount, which is short for "cat of the mountain."

The Canada lynx is closely related to the Eurasian lynx, which is found in Europe. The Eurasian lynx is bigger and preys mainly on deer.

CANADA LYNX

A snowstorm is no problem if you're a Canada lynx! In winter, a lynx grows a thick, fluffy gray coat. Its big feet, with toes that it can spread wide, also get extra fluffy. It can easily walk on top of snow with these built-in snowshoes.

Its main prey is the snowshoe hare, which is also a snow specialist. This hare turns from brown to white in winter and has large, fuzzy feet for bounding across snow. In parts of the lynx's range, snowshoe hares make up as much as 97 percent of its meals.

These two animals are so closely connected that they affect each other's population numbers in a regular cycle. About every 10 years, snowshoe hares become so plentiful in the northern part of the lynx's range that they eat most of the food in their habitat. Predators eat many of the hares while other hares starve to death from the lack of food. Hare numbers drop very low.

With fewer hares gobbling up the habitat, plants start growing back. But fewer hares also means fewer meals for predators. A year or so after hare populations drop, the numbers of lynx drop, too. Some lynx die, and females have few or no kittens.

The cycle starts all over when hare numbers rise again and then lynx populations do, too. Lynx hunt hares by following "bunny trails" that crisscross the snow like highways. They also hide along trails to jump out at prey passing by.

Scientists are wondering how this cat will respond to warming temperatures due to climate change. Will bobcats and other predators that don't rely so much on snow take over lynx habitats if snow doesn't fall in them anymore?

FACTS

FAMILY Felidae

OTHER COMMON NAMES Canadian lynx, American lynx, wildcat

SCIENTIFIC NAME *Lynx canadensis*

SIZE 26 to 42 inches (67 to 107 cm)

FOOD Snowshoe hares, rodents, birds, fish

HABITAT Northern forests made up of coniferous trees such as pine and spruce, as well as trees that lose their leaves, such as birches, willows, and aspens

RANGE Canada; Alaska; and parts of the Northwest, Great Lakes, and New England regions of the lower 48 United States

A lynx has tufts of hair on top of its ears. These tufts may help its big ears pick up sounds, or they may work like whiskers to help it detect things above its head, such as low branches.

GRAY WOLF

FACTS

FAMILY Canidae

OTHER COMMON NAMES Wolf

SCIENTIFIC NAME *Canis lupus*

SIZE 36 to 63 inches (91 to 160 cm), not including tail

FOOD Large hoofed animals such as moose, deer, and caribou, as well as smaller hoofed animals; small mammals such as rabbits and mice; carrion

HABITAT Woodlands, forests, grasslands, deserts, and cold, treeless lands called tundras in the far north

RANGE Eurasia; Canada; Alaska; parts of the northern lower 48 United States, including the northern Rocky Mountains and the Pacific Northwest and some areas of Arizona and New Mexico

What color is a gray wolf? That's not a silly question! In addition to gray, these wolves can also be brown, tan, black, red-brown, and even white.

It's hard to imagine that a poodle has much in common with a wolf—but they're actually cousins. Both dogs and wolves share a common ancestor: a species of wolf that went extinct thousands of years ago. Unlike dogs, however, wolves are wild animals that work together to hunt and kill big animals such as moose.

Wolves live in groups called packs. A pack is a big family that's usually made up of two "alphas"—a male and a female wolf—and their young born in previous years. When the alpha female gives birth, her mate and the rest of the wolves help her feed and protect the new pups.

A wolf can easily catch rabbits and other small animals on its own. But it needs its pack mates to bring down a big animal like an elk. The pack studies a herd of hoofed animals carefully, looking for one that seems weaker than the others. They'll follow the herd for miles to see which will be the easiest target before chasing it.

Wolves are very smart, as most animals that live in groups must be in order to communicate with each other and cooperate. The pack works as a team to chase and wear down larger prey before circling around it and attacking. The prey is often grabbed by the rump or nose. The wolves must be careful not to get kicked by the animal's sharp hooves or stabbed by its horns or antlers. When the prey is overcome, then the wolves dig in, eating as much as 20 pounds (9 kg) in one meal. A wolf's jaw is strong enough to crack open the leg bone of a moose.

Wolves are built for traveling long distances. They might travel about 12 miles (20 km) in one day as they hunt and patrol their territory.

A female coyote usually has five or six pups in a litter. But if she lives in a place where people hunt coyotes, she may have larger litters. With fewer adult coyotes around, there is more food for the parent coyotes and their pups, and more pups survive and grow to adulthood.

COYOTE

Coyotes are stars in some Native American stories. These coyotes are often smart, sneaky characters. Sometimes they're helpful and wise, and sometimes they're tricksters who get into trouble. In fact, they're a lot like real coyotes!

To humans, coyotes are helpful because they eat rodents that spoil crops. A single coyote can gobble up about 1,800 rodents per year. But coyotes sometimes eat lambs and other farm animals. This causes many ranchers to dislike them.

Like wolves, coyotes sometimes live in packs made up of a male, a female, and their young of different ages. Coyotes may also live alone or with a mate. A male and female coyote often stay together for years. The female gives birth to her pups in a den. She will move them from den to den if she senses danger. Her mate helps care for them. By the time they're six to eight months old, pups are able to strike out on their own.

Coyotes once lived mainly in the western United States, where they roamed prairies and sagebrush-covered lands. They didn't live where wolves did because wolves wouldn't allow it! Wolves kill coyotes if they find them in their territory because they compete for the same foods. However, when people killed off wolves across much of the United States, coyotes moved in to take their place.

These clever canines often hunt by night, though they'll hunt by day in places where people aren't around. Coyotes may take turns chasing prey so that one can catch its breath while the other runs. That way, the predators don't wear out, but the prey becomes exhausted.

FACTS

FAMILY Canidae

OTHER COMMON NAMES Prairie wolf, brush wolf, American jackal

SCIENTIFIC NAME *Canis latrans*

SIZE 32 to 37 inches (81.3 to 94 cm), not including tail

FOOD Rodents, rabbits, deer, birds, snakes, small reptiles, insects, frogs, fish, shellfish, carrion, eggs, vegetables, fruit

HABITAT Prairies, forests, woodlands, deserts, mountains, tropical areas, farmlands; can be found in towns and cities

RANGE North America, parts of Central America

Coyotes howl to keep in touch and also yip and howl when they meet after being apart for a while. Their eerie noises have earned them the nickname "song dogs."

AFRICAN WILD DOG

FACTS

FAMILY Canidae

OTHER COMMON NAMES
Cape hunting dog, painted dog, ornate wolf

SCIENTIFIC NAME *Lycaon pictus*

SIZE 29.5 to 43 inches (75 to 109 cm), not including tail

FOOD Antelopes, wildebeests, warthogs, zebras, and other hoofed animals; small mammals such as rats; birds

HABITAT Savannas, forests, woodlands, deserts

RANGE Scattered places in parts of central, eastern, northeastern, and southern Africa

African wild dogs eat animals large and small. This one has caught a rat.

With its big, batlike ears, its wildly patterned fur, and just four toes on each foot, the African wild dog looks like no other canine. Like a few other species of canids, however, African wild dogs live in packs, and all the dogs help care for pups.

African wild dogs greet and call to each other with a bubbling, twittering noise that sounds as if it could be coming from a flock of birds. A wild dog that gets separated from its pals gives a hooting call that sounds a bit like an owl's cry. This call can be heard as far as two miles (3 km) away.

A typical wild dog pack has about 10 members, but some packs have 20 or more. The dogs hunt by day, usually in the morning or evening. They'll hunt at night if the moon is very bright. When the pack spots its prey, it trots directly toward it and only starts running when the prey does. The dogs usually pick out an animal that's slower than the rest of its herd.

As the dogs run, they snap and bite at the prey to weaken it. Wild dogs aren't as fast as some of their prey, such as impalas, but they've got lots of stamina and can run for a long time. They chase their prey until it's weak from exhaustion and loss of blood. Then the dogs gobble their food quickly. If they don't, there's a good chance hyenas will come along and chase the dogs away, and take the meal for themselves.

Today wild dogs are one of the world's most endangered mammals. Only about 6,600 remain in the wild. They are threatened by habitat loss. Farmers also kill them because they fear the dogs will harm their farm animals. People are working with farmers to help them build corrals to protect their animals.

The puppies of wild dogs go out on hunts with adult dogs when they're a few months old. After the pack catches its prey, the adults let puppies eat first. Wild dogs also cough up food to feed injured pack members that can't hunt.

A black-backed jackal trots off with a bird it has just caught. The bird, however, may still have a chance to escape.

BLACK-BACKED JACKAL

Back in the early 1800s when European scientists first saw coyotes in North America, they thought it was a kind of jackal. And it's easy to see why they made this mistake: Like coyotes, jackals are smaller than wolves and very, very clever.

One of these clever canines is the black-backed jackal. Like coyotes, jackals often live in small packs that are family groups made up of a male, a female, and their pups from different years. The male and female jackals mate for life.

These little packs can hunt as a group to catch larger prey, such as antelopes, or hunt on their own to catch rabbits, birds, and insects. Jackals also howl to say "this is my territory!"

Black-backed jackals show the same ability to learn and adapt that coyotes do. In the Namib Desert, for example, jackals have learned how to hunt fur seals!

The Namib Desert is a cold, dry desert that lies along the Atlantic Ocean. Cape fur seals come ashore to rest and give birth to pups. Jackals are like a cleanup crew—they eat pups that die. But they also hunt living pups, which they kill by grabbing them by the neck or throat. It's not an easy task because the pups weigh about as much as the jackals. A strong pup can get away if it pulls the jackal into the sea. And, the jackal flees if it's attacked by the pup's angry mom!

Jackals sometimes kill goats and sheep. But jackals are also victims of predators—eagles and leopards eat them, especially the pups.

FACTS

FAMILY Canidae

OTHER COMMON NAMES
Silver-backed jackal

SCIENTIFIC NAME
Canis mesomelas

SIZE 38 to 43 inches
(96 to 110 cm), not including tail

FOOD Small mammals, reptiles, birds, insects, fruit, carrion

HABITAT Deserts, grasslands, savannas, woodlands, farmlands

RANGE Southern Africa; East Africa, including Kenya, Somalia, Ethiopia

Black-backed jackals often give birth to their pups in abandoned burrows that were dug by ant-eating aardvarks.

DINGO

FACTS

FAMILY Canidae

OTHER COMMON NAMES
Wild dog

SCIENTIFIC NAME
Canis lupus dingo

SIZE 33 to 48 inches
(86 to 123 cm), not including tail

FOOD Wallabies, kangaroos,
rabbits, rats, mice, small reptiles,
birds, insects, fruit

HABITAT Grasslands, woodlands,
deserts, tropical wetlands and
forests, mountains

RANGE Australia,
Southeast Asia

The dingo is Australia's top predator in the mammal family. It's thought to have arrived in Australia 3,000 to 5,000 years ago from parts of southeast Asia, though one study suggests that dingoes might have arrived as early as 18,300 years ago.

People used to think dingoes were just a breed of dog that happened to live in the wild. But today, they're considered to be a subspecies of wolf. (Pet dogs are, too—their scientific name is *Canis lupus familiaris*.) Dingo behavior is a lot like wolf behavior. Dingoes can hunt alone or form small family packs, like wolves. Also like wolves, they keep in touch by howling.

Dingoes are found across much of Australia, though they're mostly blocked from part of it by the world's longest fence! This fence marks a wiggly line across the middle of eastern Australia. It is 3,437 miles (5,531 km) long. It was completed in 1885 to keep rabbits out of grasslands where sheep grazed.

Today, it's known as the dingo fence. The fence failed to keep out bunnies that ate grass, but people fixed it up over time so it would keep out dingoes that ate sheep. Some scientists think the fence, or at least part of it, should come down. That's because woody shrubs are growing on large areas of grassland, which means less grass for sheep. The shrubs grow because there's a shortage of small rodents and other mammals that eat shrub seeds.

How could dingoes help? By eating the cats and foxes that eat the small mammals. Cats and foxes are not native to Australia. They were brought there by European settlers. If dingoes preyed on these smaller predators, then more mice and other little mammals would survive to feed on shrub seeds.

Dingoes once shared Australia with the thylacine, a dog-size predator that had a wolflike head and a striped hind end. It also had a pocket for its young, because it was a pouched mammal like the kangaroo and the koala bear. Thylacines are believed to be extinct.

Most dingoes are red-brown, but some desert dingoes are golden yellow. Dingoes can also be black and tan.

The fox's leap-and-pin trick for catching mice is also used by other animals, such as the maned wolf of South America and an African wildcat called the serval.

RED FOX

The red fox is famous for its method of hunting mice. It stands perfectly still when it senses a mouse. Perhaps only its big black ears will move, or its black nose will twitch as it waits.

Then, when the mouse is in just the right spot, the fox strikes. It leaps high in the air as if zapped by electricity. It brings its two front legs together and lands stiff-legged on top of the mouse. This action pins the mouse to the ground as if it had been stapled there. Then the fox can easily grab it with its jaws. A fox can leap and land on a mouse that's 16.4 feet (5 m) away!

Mice are preyed upon across huge areas of the world because red foxes have the widest distribution of any land carnivore. They exist naturally in many places, and people have set them free in places outside of their natural range.

Australia, for example, never had red foxes until the mid-1800s. That's when people from England set foxes free there so they could then hunt them on horseback. The foxes settled so well in their new land that they became a problem and killed off some of Australia's small wild species.

This ability to adapt to its environment has also helped foxes feel right at home in towns and even cities. A fox's natural habitat, however, includes grasslands and "edges"—the places between forests and grasslands.

Unlike wolves, red foxes don't form packs—but unlike dogs, male foxes do help females raise their young. A male and female fox pair up to raise young in a den that's in their territory. Their pups usually leave the territory before they are a year old, but sometimes females will stick around to help feed their mom's new litter.

FACTS

FAMILY Canidae

OTHER COMMON NAMES
Silver fox, cross fox

SCIENTIFIC NAME *Vulpes vulpes*

SIZE 35.5 to 40.5 inches
(90 to 103 cm), not including tail

FOOD Rabbits, rodents, other small mammals; birds, frogs, small reptiles, insects, worms, fruit, carrion

HABITAT Forests, grasslands, mountains, tundras, wetlands, fields, deserts, farmlands

RANGE North America, Europe, Eurasia, India, Japan, northern Africa, Australia

Red foxes can also be silver, gray, blue-gray, or black.

POLAR BEAR

FACTS

FAMILY Ursidae

OTHER COMMON NAMES
Sea bear, ice bear, white bear, nanuq (Inuit)

SCIENTIFIC NAME
Ursus maritimus

SIZE Up to 8 feet (2.5 m)

FOOD Seals, carrion, fish, seabirds

HABITAT Sea ice; also on coasts and islands

RANGE Circumpolar Arctic in Canada, the United States (Alaska), Greenland, Russia, Norway

Two young male polar bears wrestle playfully. Such fights will become serious battles in springtime when bears compete for mates.

Imagine a predator that's up to 10 feet (3 m) tall when it stands on its hind legs and can weigh more than a horse! Just such an animal prowls the icy, snowy coasts of the far north. It's the polar bear, the world's largest land predator.

Polar bears specialize in hunting seals. The bear's favorite tactic is to wait by a seal's breathing hole in the ice. It will wait for hours for a seal to pop its head into the hole. Then, *wham!* The bear grabs the seal and drags it out of the water.

A polar bear will also slowly stalk seals that are lying atop the ice. It creeps forward when the seal relaxes or sleeps. A bear will also smash open seals' snow dens to eat the pups inside.

If there are plenty of seals to hunt, a polar bear may eat just its prey's blubber and not the meat. Blubber contains more energy than meat and is more easily digested. But the meat doesn't go to waste. The little arctic foxes that follow polar bears feast on it, alongside gulls and ravens.

A polar bear needs ice that forms on seawater to hunt. It walks on ice that lasts all year long, as well as ice that forms in just the coldest months along the shore. In places such as Hudson Bay in eastern Canada, this ice melts in summer, so bears go hungry for months as they wait for ice to form again. They eat berries, bird eggs, and anything else they can find in the meantime, but they do lose weight.

Hudson Bay's ice melts earlier in spring and forms later in fall now than in the past. The bears in the area are having fewer cubs, and fewer of those grow to adulthood. By slowing climate change, we can help protect polar bear habitat to save these bears.

A polar bear can eat up to 100 pounds (45 kg) of seal blubber in one meal! That much food will keep it fueled for about a week.

Brown bears in some parts of North America are called grizzly bears. "Grizzly" refers to their fur, which contains white-tipped hairs on their back and shoulders that make the bear look "grizzled."

BROWN BEAR

Grr! **A brown bear is up to half a ton of muscle** equipped with claws as long as human fingers. These claws are great tools for digging up rodents and tearing apart logs to find insects to eat. They're also capable of killing a deer with one swat. The bear will hide, or cache, a large animal like a deer so it can feed on it for several days until every scrap of meat is eaten.

Brown bears in Alaska are famous for gathering in large numbers in places where salmon are swimming upstream to lay their eggs. The bears stand by waterfalls and shallow streams, where they grab the fish by swatting at them, hooking them with their claws, and seizing them in their massive jaws.

Brown bears also gobble up insects. Researchers have found that bears in parts of North America even climb high up mountainsides in summer to feast on army cutworm moths. A single bear can eat 40,000 moths in one day.

Though it is a carnivore, a brown bear is much more of an omnivore. It eats lots of plant foods such as roots, berries, and nuts.

Brown bears eat huge amounts of food in the fall. A bear may pack away up to 90 pounds (40 kg) in just one day. That's like eating 360 hamburgers! It eats this much to store up energy for the winter. That's when brown bears sleep very deeply, or hibernate, inside a den. They don't eat, drink, pee, or poop for months. Females, however, give birth while hibernating!

Brown bears are the most widespread bear species. Today, about half its population in the world roams across Russia.

FACTS

FAMILY Ursidae

OTHER COMMON NAMES Grizzly bear, silvertip

SCIENTIFIC NAME *Ursus arctos*

SIZE 5 to 8 feet (1.5 to 2.5 m)

FOOD Mammals, small reptiles, fish, insects, fruit, nuts, roots, leaves, grass, carrion

HABITAT Forests, woods, grasslands, mountains, tundras, coastlines, desert edges

RANGE Western North America, Siberia, Europe, Asia

The scent-detecting area of a brown bear's nose is about a hundred times bigger than yours. It can pick up the smell of prey or carrion from a mile away.

SLOTH BEAR

FACTS

FAMILY Ursidae

OTHER COMMON NAMES
Honey bear

SCIENTIFIC NAME
Melursus ursinus

SIZE 5 to 6 feet (1.5 to 1.8 m)

FOOD Ants, termites, fruit, flowers, eggs, carrion, honey

HABITAT Wet and dry tropical forests, savannas, scrublands, grasslands

RANGE India, Nepal, Sri Lanka

A sloth bear can shut its nostrils like little doors to keep ants and termites from crawling up its nose while it's raiding their nests.

Say you're hiking in a forest in India. Suddenly, you hear a weird grunting, snorting, snuffling sound in the darkness. Who's vacuuming rugs among the trees in the middle of the night? That's no vacuum—what you hear is the sound of a sloth bear having dinner.

Sloth bears are the only bears that eat mainly ants and termites. They eat a lot of fruit when fruit is plentiful, but for the rest of the year, ants and termites top the bears' menu.

A sloth bear's snout is adapted for a life of eating insects. The bear has floppy lips and a gap between its upper front teeth. The roof of its mouth is long and arched. These features help the bear suck up insects by turning its mouth into a vacuum tube. All the bear has to do is dig into a termite mound or anthill with its long claws and press its mouth and lips around the opening. Then, *slurp!* It noisily sucks up insects.

Sloth bears use their claws not only to dig up insects but also to protect themselves from predators such as tigers and jackals.

A sloth bear spends eight to 14 hours a day "working" to find food. It's certainly not "slothful," or lazy, so why is it called a sloth bear? It's all a case of mistaken identity.

In 1791, a British scientist named George Shaw wrote about the bear, which he thought was a kind of sloth—a very slow-moving rain forest animal that hangs upside down from branches. The name stuck even though scientists soon figured out that these animals were not sloths, but bears.

Sloth bears are the only bears that regularly carry their cubs on their backs. Many other animals that eat ants and termites, such as giant anteaters, tote their offspring this way, too.

Spotted hyenas look a bit like dogs, but they're actually more closely related to cats and to weasel-like animals called civets. Female spotted hyenas are bigger than males. They're also the bosses in hyena clans.

SPOTTED HYENA

It takes a very strong bite to crack an animal leg bone in two. For a spotted hyena, this challenge is like snapping toothpicks! It has incredibly powerful jaws and teeth. Researchers have seen a spotted hyena crunch a giraffe bone that was 2.8 inches (7 cm) wide!

When a spotted hyena eats its prey, there's very little it doesn't swallow. It gulps down not only meat but also skin, bones, hooves, and horns. It can eat up to 40 pounds (18 kg) in just one meal! Hyenas don't gobble up these supersize meals because they're greedy. They just never know when their next meal might be. Plus, there's always a chance that lions will come along, chase away the hyenas, and steal their prey, leaving nothing but bones and skin for the hyenas to eat.

The fact that lions steal from hyenas often surprises people, because it was once thought that hyenas were scavengers that ate leftovers from lions' meals. But hyenas are actually very capable predators.

A clan, or group, of hyenas can work like a team to take down prey, just as wolf packs do. A big clan, which may include about 80 hyenas, can hunt large prey such as wildebeests, zebras, and African buffalo. A smaller clan tackles smaller prey such as warthogs and gazelles. A hyena hunting on its own can catch rabbits, foxes, and birds.

Hyenas and humans don't always get along, because hyenas can prey on sheep and cattle. But they also get respect. In a few African cities, hyenas are even welcomed because their big appetites help clean up food waste and other trash.

FACTS

FAMILY Hyaenidae

OTHER COMMON NAMES Laughing hyena

SCIENTIFIC NAME *Crocuta crocuta*

SIZE 34 to 59 inches (86 to 150 cm)

FOOD Mammals, birds, lizards, snakes, insects, ostrich eggs, carrion, fruit, plants

HABITAT Savannas, grasslands, woodlands, forest edges, mountains, drylands

RANGE Sub-Saharan Africa

A spotted hyena can run up to 37 miles an hour (60 km/h).

AARDWOLF

FACTS

FAMILY Hyaenidae

OTHER COMMON NAMES
Maned jackal, gray jackal

SCIENTIFIC NAME
Proteles cristata

SIZE 22 to 31 inches (55 to 80 cm), not including tail

FOOD Termites, ants

HABITAT Grasslands, scrublands, savannas

RANGE Eastern, northeastern, and southern Africa

An aardwolf can eat up to 300,000 termites in just one night.

You'll never find aardwolves hunting as a pack.
That's because they don't prey on big mammals. A hungry aardwolf has only its favorite meal in mind: termites.

Even though an aardwolf has big canine teeth in its powerful jaws, it doesn't need them to eat termites. Instead, it uses its wide, sticky tongue to slurp them up. And it doesn't just eat any old termite—an aardwolf hones in on a species called harvester termites. It finds these termites collecting grass on dry ground, and simply licks them off the soil. If it can't find harvester termites, it will eat other species.

Aardwolves usually hunt at night because that's when its preferred kind of termites is active. They also usually feed alone. Even a male and female that are paired up will eat separately so they don't compete with each other for food.

Eating termites off dusty soil sounds as if it would leave an aardwolf with a dry mouth, but an aardwolf doesn't usually need to drink water. It gets the water it needs from the termites' plump bodies.

Both the male and female aardwolf care for cubs, which are born in a den. The male protects the cubs from jackals, which are predators of aardwolves. He also guards the den while his mate goes off to feed. An aardwolf cub starts snacking on termites when it's about nine weeks old.

In the past, some farmers killed aardwolves because they thought the animals were eating their lambs, chickens, or eggs. They were probably confusing aardwolves with hyenas or jackals. Today, most people realize that aardwolves pose no harm. The use of insecticides, however, is a threat to their survival.

The aardwolf's name means "earth wolf" in the Afrikaans language. It is also called by the long name "maanhaar-jackal," which means "mane hair jackal." This name was inspired by the way an aardwolf's hair stands up on its back when it feels angry or threatened.

81

Researchers once observed a honey badger that ate enough snakes to measure a total of 30 feet (9.1 m) in just three days.

HONEY BADGER

The honey badger has a sweet name, but it's far from cuddly! It is a tough little predator that's been known to stand up to lions. It's one of Earth's most fearless creatures.

Few other small animals would dare to attack venomous snakes and eat them, but the honey badger does. It seizes the snake behind its head to kill it. Even if it's bitten, the honey badger seems to shrug off the venom's deadly effects. Once the snake is dead, the honey badger chomps on it as if it's a very long hot dog, starting with the head.

A honey badger spends much of its time searching for things to eat. It pokes its head into burrows to sniff for mice and rats. It climbs up trees to hunt snakes and goes underwater to seek turtles. It barges into beehives to eat young bees, called larvae, as well as honey (that's what puts the "honey" in "honey badger").

As the honey badger hunts, it's often watched by other predators. These include jackals and birds called chanting goshawks, which will catch any prey that escapes the honey badger's clutches.

Some animals, such as lions, leopards, and spotted hyenas, will attack honey badgers themselves. But these brave animals charge at their attackers, bite, let loose a terrible smell, and make loud hissing noises.

If caught, a honey badger can twist inside its thick, loose-fitting skin, making it hard for a predator to hold it.

FACTS

FAMILY Mustelidae

OTHER COMMON NAMES Ratel

SCIENTIFIC NAME *Mellivora capensis*

SIZE Up to 2.4 feet (73 cm)

FOOD Small mammals, rodents, birds, snakes, small reptiles, frogs, insects, carrion, eggs, fruit, roots, plants

HABITAT Savannas, drylands, forests, woods

RANGE Africa, Middle East, India

A honey badger has a gland near its tail that produces a smelly fluid. It uses the fluid to mark its territory with its scent. It will also release this fluid if it is attacked or scared.

FOSSA

FACTS

FAMILY Eupleridae

OTHER COMMON NAMES Fosa

SCIENTIFIC NAME
Cryptoprocta ferox

SIZE 23.5 to 30 inches
(60 to 76 cm), not including tail

FOOD Lemurs, rodents, birds,
small reptiles, frogs, fish

HABITAT Dry forests, rain forests

RANGE Madagascar

Many of the animals found on Madagascar, an island about the size of Texas in the United States, live nowhere else. Madagascar lies in the Indian Ocean about 250 miles (400 km) from Africa's coast. Here is where you'll find remarkable creatures such as tiny chameleons that look like leaves and long-legged lemurs leaping in the trees.

You'll also find the fossa—a carnivore that looks like a cross between a cat and a weasel. Like a weasel, it has small, rounded ears and a long, slim body. Like a cat, it can pull in its claws when it's not using them to climb or grab prey. A tail that measures up to two feet (70 cm) helps it balance as it scrambles through treetops in pursuit of its main food, lemurs.

These nimble predators start life in a den as tiny, toothless pups with white hair. There they stay for up to five months. After pups leave the den, they stay with their mom for up to eight months. They're not full-grown until they're between two and three years old, and can start breeding a year or so later.

Fossas are the top predators in Madagascar, though people have hunted them since discovering the island about 2,000 years ago. Today, dogs introduced by humans also go after fossas.

But the biggest threat faced by fossas is the same one faced by their prey: deforestation, or the cutting down of forests. The forests are cut by farmers, logging and mining companies, and people cutting trees to make charcoal for use as fuel. Madagascar today has only about 10 percent of the forest that once covered its hills and mountains.

How can deforestation be stopped? Creating protected areas and enforcing laws about land use are two solutions. Another effort is practicing sustainability. That means using resources in a way that doesn't deplete them and also makes sure people—and wildlife—will have the clean air, water, and habitat they need to survive in the future.

A fossa's flexible ankle joints, strong legs, and sharp claws enable it to zip right up tree trunks like a squirrel. It can even climb down them headfirst.

A fossa looks catlike, but it doesn't walk on its toes like a cat. It walks on flat feet like a bear when it's on the ground.

Wolverines often hide leftovers from meals and mark the hiding places with a strong, musky scent that says "Paws off!" That's how they've earned nicknames such as "stink bear" and "skunk bear." A favorite storage place for food is a deep snowbank, which works like a freezer to keep the meat from going bad. A wolverine's jaws are strong enough to gnaw on this frozen food.

WOLVERINE

The wolverine is a small but tough predator that's often described as ferocious. It weighs less than your average friendly Labrador retriever, but it's fierce enough to charge a cougar!

Wolverines are always ready to eat. They live in harsh habitats with long, cold winters, so they need to feed to keep up their energy supply. They'll wander nearly 20 miles (32 km) in a day looking for things to eat.

Carrion is a favorite and very important food for wolverines, but they are also able to catch their own prey. They can easily kill small animals. In winter, they'll even dig up the dens of hibernating animals to eat them as they sleep. Wolverines will also attack larger animals, especially if they are injured, sick, old, or trapped in snow.

Snow is important to wolverines, which are adapted for a life in the fluffy white stuff. Thick fur keeps them warm. Short legs with wide paws help them walk on snow. Strong, curved claws help them climb snowy cliffs. Female wolverines dig snow tunnels that lead to cozy dens where they give birth to their kits.

The wolverine's need for snow makes global climate change a threat to this species. Warmer temperatures in northern regions could result in less snow and less habitat for these animals.

In parts of Europe, wolverines have been trapped and hunted because they prey on sheep and on reindeer owned by herders. That's made this naturally rare animal even harder to find in many places. In North America, wolverines are doing okay in some places, such as Alaska and western Canada, but just hanging on in other places, such as parts of the Rocky Mountains in the United States. Wildlife scientists are studying them so we can better understand what wolverines need to survive.

FACTS

FAMILY Mustelidae

OTHER COMMON NAMES Glutton, skunk bear, stink bear, woods devil, carcajou

SCIENTIFIC NAME *Gulo gulo*

SIZE 26 to 34 inches (66 to 86 cm), not including tail

FOOD Moose, reindeer, caribou, and other deer; small mammals; rodents; birds; fish; eggs; roots; berries; carrion

HABITAT Forests, tundras, mountains

RANGE Scandinavia, Russia, Canada, Alaska and western United States

A wolverine can smell a dead animal that's buried under 20 feet (6 m) of snow.

ZORILLA

FACTS

FAMILY Mustelidae

OTHER COMMON NAMES
African skunk, striped polecat, striped weasel, zorille

SCIENTIFIC NAME
Ictonyx striatus

SIZE 11 to 15 inches (28 to 38 cm), not including tail

FOOD Insects, frogs, small reptiles, birds, eggs, rodents

HABITAT Grasslands, savannas, thornbush, rocky places, forests, scrub deserts, farmlands

RANGE Central Africa, excluding the Congo Basin

It looks like a skunk. It's about the same size as a skunk. It sprays stinky musk like a skunk, too. But it's not a skunk—it's the zorilla, a member of the weasel family that lives in Africa.

A zorilla prefers to mind its own business, but it is ready to defend itself if attacked. First, it signals a warning with a raised, fluffed-up tail and angry growls. If the predator keeps bugging it, the zorilla whips around its hind end and sprays a terrible-smelling musk.

If raising a stink doesn't repel the predator, the zorilla plays dead. Many predators aren't interested in dead animals that they didn't kill themselves. In addition, any predator that picks up the "dead" zorilla will get a mouthful of nasty-tasting musky fur and probably drop it!

A zorilla spends its nights feeding on small rodents and insects such as beetles and grasshoppers. Its sturdy claws help it dig up insects and mice in burrows. Many farmers appreciate having zorillas prowl their farmlands because they eat beetles that harm the roots of plants, as well as rodents that eat crops. But they are wary of them, too, because zorillas will also kill chickens.

Zorillas live in many habitats and are widespread in Africa, so they're not endangered. Their main enemies in some places are vehicles—zorillas that walk on roads at night can get hit by cars.

The zorilla's spray can be smelled up to half a mile (0.8 km) away. The odor is so strong that it can repel lions. Even vultures, which eat carrion, often avoid feeding on dead zorillas. In parts of Africa, the zorilla is called stinkmuishond, which means "stink mouse dog" in the Afrikaans language.

A zorilla's tail can be nearly as long as its head and body.

Badgers will eagerly eat snakes. They have some resistance to the snake's deadly venom, so it often has no effect on them.

AMERICAN BADGER

Dig, dig, dig! That's what badgers do. A badger's big front paws are equipped with long, strong claws, which it uses to dig up prey. Its main meals are rodents that live in burrows, such as ground squirrels, prairie dogs, rats, and mice. A hungry badger quickly unearths these little animals and eats them. If they're not at home, it may hide in the dug-out burrow and wait for them to return.

If a coyote sees a badger digging up rodent burrows, it may hang around and watch. It knows that frightened rodents may dash out of the burrow to escape the badger—only to end up in the coyote's jaws.

A badger also digs its own dens and burrows. It uses them in many ways. A badger naps in one by day. It dozes in a den during very cold spells in winter. A female gives birth in a den lined with grass. If a predator threatens a badger, it will back into a burrow so that its sharp claws and snarling face are turned toward its attacker. It can then back farther into the burrow and plug it up with dirt.

If caught, a badger fights back fiercely. It's protected by thick fur and tough, loose-fitting skin, so it can spin around and claw and bite its attacker. A predator doesn't want to be injured by its prey, so it's likely to let go of a snarling, twisting creature with sharp claws.

American badgers are very distantly related to European badgers. The two animals have similar gray fur and markings, but the European badger's favorite meal isn't a rodent—it's earthworms!

FACTS

FAMILY Mustelidae

OTHER COMMON NAMES Badger, North American badger

SCIENTIFIC NAME *Taxidea taxus*

SIZE 16.5 to 29.9 inches (42 to 76 cm), not including tail

FOOD Rodents, birds, snakes, lizards, frogs, toads, insects, scorpions, worms, carrion

HABITAT Grasslands, fields, pastures

RANGE Western and central United States, southern Canada, northern and central Mexico

The badger is the official state animal of Wisconsin. According to legend, it got this name because early miners in Wisconsin lived like "badgers" in old mines.

BLACK-FOOTED FERRET

FACTS

FAMILY Mustelidae

OTHER COMMON NAMES None

SCIENTIFIC NAME
Mustela nigripes

SIZE 15 to 20 inches (38 to 50 cm), not including tail

FOOD Prairie dogs, ground squirrels, mice, and other rodents

HABITAT Prairie dog towns in grasslands

RANGE Scattered sites across west-central North America

The black-footed ferret looks like a bandit in a mask. Its slim body lets it zip in and out of burrows of prairie dogs, which are its main prey. About 90 percent of a ferret's meals consist of prairie dog. The ferrets live in empty prairie dog burrows, too. Ferrets, in turn, are eaten by animals such as golden eagles and coyotes.

Black-footed ferrets once lived in grasslands that stretched from southern Canada to northern Mexico. But then many grasslands were turned into farms and ranches. People viewed prairie dogs as pests. They poisoned entire colonies. Without prairie dogs to eat, the ferrets died, too.

By 1978, black-footed ferrets were thought to be extinct. But then, in the fall of 1981, a ranch dog named Shep dropped a mysterious creature on its owner's doorstep in Wyoming. You guessed it: It was a black-footed ferret! Scientists quickly found the prairie dog colony it came from and discovered that a small number of ferrets were living there.

Today, black-footed ferrets are still rare and endangered, but their numbers are up. Several hundred ferrets live in the wild, with a few hundred more in captive breeding programs.

Scientists are experimenting with using drones to help ferrets fight off a disease called plague. The drones drop blobs of a peanut-butter mixture across prairie dog colonies for the animals to eat. The blobs contain a vaccine, a substance that helps the body fight off diseases.

Black-footed ferrets are North America's only naturally existing, or native, species of ferret.

The mongoose family includes meerkats, which live in southern Africa. Meerkats live in large family groups. They gang up to kill snakes that would otherwise slip into their burrows to eat them.

COMMON MONGOOSE

If you've ever read *The Jungle Book,* **you've met** the common mongoose. The author, Rudyard Kipling, wrote about these fierce little animals in a story called "Rikki-Tikki-Tavi." In it, he describes the mongoose as "rather like a little cat in his fur and his tail, but quite like a weasel in his head and his habits."

For a mongoose, those habits include zipping around in search of food. A mongoose is what's known as an "opportunistic" feeder, which means it eats anything it finds that's edible. That includes venomous snakes such as cobras.

A mongoose in battle with a cobra looks as if it's locked in a deadly dance. It leaps back and forth quickly as the cobra strikes at it with its fangs. The cobra normally misses, but even if it lands a bite, the mongoose is usually just fine, thanks to its thick coat. Its body also resists the effects of venom. When the snake gets tired, the mongoose finally makes its move. It lunges at the cobra and bites its head.

A mongoose also knows how to handle other difficult foods, such as scorpions. It picks up these stinging animals in its front paws and hurls them backward between its hind legs again and again to smash them. It also cracks open large bird eggs in this way by flinging them against a rock or a wall.

Scientists have found that in some mongoose species, babies learn by copying their mom's behavior. A mongoose's know-how may also be partly due to instinct, which is behavior that an animal is born knowing. The animal's instinct may simply be the urge to do something, but learning helps it find out how. Tame mongooses that have never seen a snake, for example, have been known to expertly attack a rubber one.

FACTS

FAMILY Herpestidae

OTHER COMMON NAMES Gray mongoose, Indian gray mongoose

SCIENTIFIC NAME *Herpestes edwardsii*

SIZE 29 to 32 inches (73 to 81 cm), not including tail

FOOD Mice, birds, rats, snakes, lizards, frogs, fish, insects, spiders, scorpions, crabs, centipedes, eggs, plants, fruits, berries, roots

HABITAT Dry forests, scrublands, grasslands, farmlands

RANGE India, Nepal, Sri Lanka, Pakistan, Bhutan, Bangladesh, and other areas in western Asia

A common mongoose can roll up into a ball like an armadillo or a hedgehog to protect itself.

PYGMY SHREW

FAMILY Soricidae

OTHER COMMON NAMES
American pygmy shrew

SCIENTIFIC NAME *Sorex hoyi*

SIZE 1.5 to 2 inches (3.8 to 5 cm), not including tail

FOOD Insects, insect larvae, spiders, worms, snails, seeds, berries

HABITAT Forests, woodlands, fields, bogs, marshes, swamps

RANGE Canada, Alaska, northern Rocky Mountains, Great Lakes region, New England, and Appalachian Mountains; scattered populations in southern Rocky Mountains

The pygmy shrew is one of the world's smallest mammals. It weighs about as much as a dime. It seems as if it would be just a snack for the bigger predators in this book.

Owls, hawks, weasels, foxes, snakes, and other animals certainly do eat pygmy shrews. But the tiny shrew itself is a fierce predator for its size. Just ask the insects and other invertebrates that it eats.

A pygmy shrew is a mighty hunter because it is constantly hungry. Every day, it must eat an amount of food that weighs as much as it does. If it doesn't eat for an hour, it can die. This huge appetite is caused by the shrew's small size. Because it's little, it has a larger surface, or skin, area for its size than a bigger animal does. That means it loses more body heat for its size than, say, you do. So the shrew has to eat a lot of food to get the energy it needs to stay warm and to move.

It also has to work hard to keep its body's furnace running. A shrew breathes in and out about 800 times a minute and its heart patters away as much as 1,200 beats per minute—and that's when it's taking a break! (For comparison, your heart beats about 70 to 110 times a minute.)

Some of the pygmy shrew's energy goes into digging in soil to find food. It also uses tunnels dug by other animals, such as moles. It scurries along the tunnels to search for worms and other small animals to eat. It hears well and also possesses a sharp sense of smell, so it can easily find food in the dark.

A pygmy shrew is almost always on the prowl for food. Its long nose twitches nonstop as it scurries about, sniffing for something to eat.

A pygmy shrew barely even stops looking for food to sleep. Instead, it takes short naps that last just a few minutes.

Tasmanian devils were probably once hunted by thylacines, predators that are now considered extinct (though every few years reports pop up claiming a sighting of one). Today, devils are the top predator in Tasmania. But they also help protect other species that live there because they will eat the young of invasive predators such as cats and foxes, which never existed naturally on the island.

TASMANIAN DEVIL

When European explorers visited Tasmania in the late 1700s and heard screams and growls in the dark, they imagined it was the sound of devils! The noises were actually just the squabbles of a particular predator. But the name stuck, and the animals are still called Tasmanian devils today.

Tasmanian devils look about as quarrelsome as they sound. They have stocky bodies like bulldogs and big heads. They can open their jaws very wide, revealing rows of pointy teeth.

This creatures lives alone most of the time. It sleeps by day and comes out at night to feed. Dead animals are favorite meals because obviously they're easy pickings—no killing required. A large carcass, however, attracts many devils. They growl and screech at each other as they vie for the best spots at the feast.

Like kangaroos and koalas, the devil is a marsupial—an animal that gives birth to tiny, undeveloped young that finish growing inside a pouch. A female devil gives birth to as many as 30 babies at a time, each one no bigger than a raisin. They crawl along her fur and into her pouch. But only four of them will survive, because there are only four milk-producing nipples inside the pouch.

Devils once lived across Australia, but now live only on the nearby island of Tasmania. Scientists think that dingoes (pp. 68–69) were the main cause of their extinction in Australia. Ranchers and farmers tried to wipe out devils on Tasmania, but the animals became protected by law in 1941 because they were becoming rare.

FACTS

FAMILY Dasyuridae

OTHER COMMON NAMES None

SCIENTIFIC NAME *Sarcophilus harrisii*

SIZE 23 to 26 inches (57 to 65 cm), not including tail

FOOD Mammals, birds, reptiles, frogs, fish, insects, grubs, carrion

HABITAT Forests, woodlands, coastal scrublands, farmlands

RANGE Tasmania

Tasmanian devils, like other marsupials, store fat in their tails. Their bodies can use this fat when food is hard to find.

SPOTTED-TAIL QUOLL

FACTS

FAMILY Dasyuridae

OTHER COMMON NAMES
Spot-tailed quoll, tiger cat, tiger quoll

SCIENTIFIC NAME
Dasyurus maculatus

SIZE 14 to 30 inches (35 to 76 cm), not including tail

FOOD Mammals, birds, reptiles, insects, spiders, scorpions, crayfish, eggs, carrion

HABITAT Forests, rain forests, woodlands, coastal scrub, riversides, rocky outcrops

RANGE Eastern Australia, Tasmania

Scientists who study quolls can easily find quoll poo (called scat) in places where there are a lot of quolls. Special dogs, called wildlife sniffer dogs, are trained to find quoll poo.

Thylacines and Tasmanian devils (see p. 98) are long gone from the island continent of Australia. That leaves the spotted-tail quoll as the largest natural carnivore surviving there. (Dingoes are much bigger, but they were brought to Australia by people.)

At night, the spotted-tail quoll prowls among rocks, in ditches, and up in trees to find its dinner. It may also hunt by day, which is when it's most likely to find possums. Possums are active at night and spend the day sleeping in their treetop nests. The quoll kills possums and other prey, such as rabbits, with a bite to the back of the head. When a quoll is not dabbling in daytime hunting, it curls up in a den in a hollow log or among rocks.

Female quolls also use dens as places to stow their young. Newborn baby quolls develop for 8 to 10 weeks in their mom's pouch. After that, they're tucked into a grassy nest in the den when the female goes hunting. If she decides to move to a new den, she totes the little ones with her on her back.

Scientists who research spotted-tail quolls have an interesting way to find out about where they live and what they eat: They visit quoll bathrooms! Quolls living in the same place use a shared area to poop and pee. These areas are called latrines. Samples can easily be collected and analyzed to find out a lot about the quolls, such as the numbers of males and females, their reproductive cycles, and what they eat.

Researching these animals is important work because spotted-tail quolls are endangered in parts of Australia. Scientists are concerned about the ones in Tasmania, too.

Spotted-tail quolls are also called tiger quolls even though they're obviously not striped like tigers. The name probably comes from the fierce hissing sounds quolls make when they're upset.

Brazilian free-tailed bats were once thought to fly no faster than 60 miles an hour (96.5 km/h). A recent study, however, found that they can actually zip at speeds up to 100 miles an hour (160 km/h)! That's quite a bit faster than the average speed of a car on a highway.

BRAZILIAN FREE-TAILED BAT

The sky is a seething mass of flapping wings on summer evenings outside Bracken Cave in Texas. That's when millions of Brazilian free-tailed bats pour out of the cave, whirling up into the sky to start the nightly hunt for flying insects.

Brazilian free-tailed bats find insects by using sound. They make very high-pitched calls as they fly, then listen for echoes bouncing back to their ears. They can figure out the distance to an object by how long it takes the echoes to reach them.

A bat can pinpoint a tiny flying insect using this process, called echolocation. It then seizes the insect with its mouth or scoops it up with a wing or its tail before grabbing it with its teeth.

Bats must eat lots of insects every night, especially if they are moms with babies waiting for them back in the cave. As mammals, female bats must eat well in order to make milk for their nursing pups. A single bat can eat hundreds of moths, beetles, and other insects. It's estimated that the 20 million bats that zoom out of Bracken Cave gobble up more than 250 tons (227 t) of insects in one night!

At summer's end, the caves get quieter. Most Brazilian free-tailed bats in the United States migrate to Central and South America for the winter. The hawks, owls, skunks, and snakes that wait for the bats to exit the cave each night go find other prey to catch.

FACTS

FAMILY Molossidae

OTHER COMMON NAMES Mexican free-tailed bat, guano bat

SCIENTIFIC NAME *Tadarida brasiliensis*

SIZE 3.5 to 4.5 inches (9 to 11 cm), not including tail

FOOD Insects

HABITAT Caves and other shelters in a wide variety of habitats

RANGE Mexico, western and southern United States, Central America, South America, Caribbean

Bats can really pack themselves into small spaces. As many as 200 or more adult bats can cram into just one square foot (.09 sq m) of cave-wall space when the bats rest by day.

LEOPARD SEAL

FACTS

FAMILY Phocidae

OTHER COMMON NAMES
Sea leopard

SCIENTIFIC NAME
Hydrurga leptonyx

SIZE 10 to 11.5 feet (3 to 3.5 m)

FOOD Penguins, seals, fish, squid, krill, carrion

HABITAT Ice floes, cold ocean waters

RANGE Atlantic Ocean, Indian Ocean, Pacific Ocean around Antarctica

Both male and female leopard seals "sing" underwater during the breeding season. Their songs sound like moans and trills. The seals may do this to find mates.

Penguins look before they leap off the ice into the freezing waters around Antartica. That's because predators lurk in those waters, just waiting to sink their teeth into these tasty, plump birds. One of the most ferocious of those predators is the leopard seal.

Leopard seals prowl along the edges of the pack ice—slabs of frozen seawater along Antarctica's coast. They are the only seals that regularly hunt warm-blooded animals. About half of their meals are made up of penguins and the pups of other species of seals. The rest of their food consists of fish, squid, and small, shrimplike animals called krill.

A leopard seal doesn't look as cuddly as many seals do. Its head is more like an alligator's, with huge jaws that gape wide to reveal daggerlike fangs. They have long, thin bodies so they can slip swiftly through the water. Their extra-long front flippers help them change direction quickly as they zip after prey.

A leopard seal that catches a penguin or another species of seal has a dramatic way of killing and eating it. It holds the prey by the head or hind end above the water's surface. Then the seal flings its head and neck so that its prey whips through the air before slamming into the ocean's surface. This action removes the skin and breaks up the body, which the seal quickly gobbles up.

To feed on animals as small as krill, a leopard seal uses the teeth behind its fangs. It sucks in water as if it were drinking from a straw. Then the water is forced out of its mouth through its back teeth, which are shaped and positioned so that they lock together to form a sieve.

Paul Nicklen has taken pictures all over the world, including off the coast of Antarctica. There, he swam in frigid waters to capture images of leopard seals. People had warned him that these predators might attack him. Instead, to his amazement, a huge female seal kept trying to feed him penguins! She brought him live birds, and then dead ones. She kept up this behavior for four days and never tried to harm him. (Experts recommend that people still avoid swimming with leopard seals, as this may just have been a case of unusual behavior.)

Male elephant seals' noses enlarge and become inflatable when they're about seven years old. This big nose helps the males make loud grunting, trumpeting noises during breeding season.

NORTHERN ELEPHANT SEAL

Northern elephant seals look like giant gray sausages on land. The blubber that keeps them warm in frigid oceans makes them clumsy and odd-looking on shore. But in the water, an elephant seal turns into a strong, graceful swimmer that can dive as deep as 5,692 feet (1,735 m) to catch prey.

Northern elephant seals are truly most at home in the ocean. They even make two long-distance migrations per year—and spend almost 90 percent of that time underwater.

The first migration takes the seals from breeding grounds on beaches in Mexico and California all the way up north to Alaska and the northern Pacific Ocean. There the seals feast on squid, fish, and other prey.

Then the seals turn around and swim all the way back to their breeding colonies. This time, the seals come ashore to shed, or molt, their fur as well as the top layer of their skin. The skin and fur don't all fall off at once—they drop off in sheets, leaving the seals looking patchy and scruffy.

After molting, the seals have new coats of fur. They return to the ocean and swim back to the feeding grounds. They'll be back in six months, when it's time to raise seal pups again. All told, the seals' trips add up to 21,000 miles (33,800 km) in a year.

FACTS

FAMILY Phocidae

OTHER COMMON NAMES Sea elephant

SCIENTIFIC NAME *Mirounga angustirostris*

SIZE 10 to 13 feet (3 to 4 m)

FOOD Squid, octopuses, fish, rays, sharks

HABITAT Sandy beaches, near shores, and open ocean waters

RANGE Central and eastern Pacific Ocean from Baja California to Gulf of Alaska

A male elephant seal can be three to four times as heavy as a female. They can weigh as much as 4,400 pounds (2,000 kg). That's about as much as a minivan!

Some orcas in South America "beach" themselves to hunt. This one rides ashore on a wave and prepares to seize its prey, a young sea lion. It will lurch back into deep water with its catch.

ORCA

What has a really big brain, can swim at speeds of up to 30 miles an hour (48 km/h), and has jaws filled with teeth up to four inches (10 cm) long? It's the orca—a predator in the dolphin family that's so awesome it can kill and eat great white sharks.

Imagine an orca teaming up with a whole pack, or pod, of its kind. Orcas travel in family groups led by the females and hunt like a wolf pack. Together, they use their big brains as well as their power to catch prey using different tactics.

In Antarctica, for example, orcas charge together at seals sitting on ice floes. Their charge creates waves. The waves rush over the floe as the orcas dive underneath it. The rushing water washes the seals off the floe and into the sea, where they become an easy catch for the orcas.

Orcas also hunt together to herd small fish into a clump. Then they use their tails to strike at the fish, which stuns them and makes them easier to catch. Herding also comes in handy when orcas force small whales to swim near shore and get stuck in shallow water. Then the orcas can attack them more easily.

Orcas will even go after big whales such as blue whales and humpbacks. The orcas ram the whale with their heads. They bite it, tug at it, and leap on its back. Finally their huge prey runs out of energy and may even drown, becoming a gigantic floating feast. And sea lions on shore in parts of South America get a shock when orcas lunge out of the water to grab them.

Though orcas prey on many different animals, they're known to specialize on certain prey. In the eastern North Pacific, some orcas feed mainly on salmon. Other groups of orcas in the same waters hunt mainly seals and whales.

FACTS

FAMILY Delphinidae

OTHER COMMON NAMES
Killer whale, grampus, blackfish

SCIENTIFIC NAME *Orcinus orca*

SIZE Up to 33 feet (10 m)

FOOD Fish (including sharks), squid, porpoises, dolphins, small whales, whale calves, seals, sea lions, sea turtles, seabirds

HABITAT Near shores and open oceans

RANGE Worldwide in all oceans, most abundant in North Atlantic and North Pacific and near Antarctica

To catch a shark, an orca shoves it to the ocean's surface using its tail. Then it smacks the shark with its tail, flips it over, and grabs it before it can start moving again.

A sperm whale's head can make up one-third of its total length. Inside that big head is a brain that may weigh 17 pounds (7.7 kg)—the largest of any animal. Also in the head is a waxy substance called spermaceti. That's the source of the whale's name. It is thought that the spermaceti helps the whale aim the sounds it uses to find prey.

SPERM WHALE

Sperm whales are champion deep-sea divers.
They've been recorded diving as deep as 7,382 feet (2,250 m) beneath the waves. Much of their life is still a mystery.

But even as far back as the late 1700s, whalers—men who hunted whales for the oil in their blubber—had a good idea of one thing sperm whales were up to. The whalers found beaks in the whales' stomachs as well as long tentacles lined with suckers. They realized that sperm whales were hunting squid.

Today, scientists find out how sperm whales live using technology such as deep-sea cameras, recording equipment, and submersibles.

Using these tools, scientists have learned that the deep sea contains not only giant squid measuring up to 60 feet (18 m) long, but also colossal squid, which are a bit bigger. Sperm whales eat these huge squid and gobble up much smaller squid, too, as well as octopuses and other prey.

In recent years, researchers have discovered that sperm whales make noises that help them find squid—even ones as small as a shoe. A whale's clicks and clangs are reflected by a squid's body back to the whale. The echoes provide clues to the squid's location—this is called echolocation. Then the whale swoops toward the squid. It twists its body at the last second and sucks the squid into its mouth from as far as 3 feet (1 m) away.

This predatory behavior allows a sperm whale to pick out a squid no bigger than a loaf of bread from a mile (1.6 km) away. It can eat more than a ton (0.9 t) of squid and fish in just one day!

FACTS

FAMILY Physeteridae

OTHER COMMON NAMES
Cachelot, spermacet whale, pot whale

SCIENTIFIC NAME
Physeter macrocephalus

SIZE 49 to 59 feet (15 to 18 m)

FOOD Squid, sharks, skates, fish

HABITAT Oceans

RANGE Nearly worldwide in all oceans

A sperm whale has 20 to 26 cone-shaped teeth in each side of its lower jaw. Each tooth can weigh up to two pounds (0.9 kg).

BEAKS, FEET & TREMENDOUS TALONS

A bald eagle can carry a fish that weighs about a third of its own body weight. If it snags a fish too heavy to lift, it will often use its wings to row to shore, rather than let go of its prey.

ALL ABOUT PREDATORY BIRDS

Some of Earth's most amazing predators are birds.
They don't have fangs—birds don't have any teeth at all—but they get the job done with a huge variety of beaks, claws, and strength.

Any bird that snaps up aphids and caterpillars is a predator—especially in the eyes of insects. When scientists talk about birds of prey, however, they're referring to certain kinds of birds. They're talking about raptors—birds that seize prey with their feet. Eagles, hawks, falcons, and owls are examples of raptors. Raptors' feet are adapted with sharp claws, called talons, and incredible gripping strength for killing prey. Their beaks are hooked or sharply edged to tear prey apart.

But raptors aren't the only birds that hunt prey larger than an insect. Many seabirds, for example, hunt for fish. Adaptations for the fishing life show up in their bodies and bills. Ducks called mergansers, for example, have notches in their beaks for holding on to slippery fish. Loons have legs set far back on their bodies, which work well as paddles for swimming underwater.

All birds, no matter what they eat, play important roles in their habitats. You can see this just by glancing at some numbers. For example, a barn owl eats about three to four rodents a night—nearly 1,500 in a single year. Rodents reproduce rapidly, and without raptors around to keep them in check, they'd eat so many plants and seeds that they'd ruin their own habitat. This, in turn, would harm other animals that depend on that habitat, too.

GANNET
Morus bassanus

The northern gannet eats fish. A gannet flies high above the ocean and then dives in at speeds up to 60 miles an hour (96.5 km/h). That's as fast as a car on a highway. It folds its wings as it slices into the water like an arrow. Most animals would be knocked out upon hitting the water at that speed, but a gannet has air sacs in its chest and neck to help cushion the shock.

SNAIL KITE
Rostrhamus sociabilis

The snail kite is an odd kind of raptor. It feeds mainly on snails—and usually just one species, the apple snail. The kite soars over marshes to pluck snails off plants with its feet. It takes the snail to a perch and carefully picks the snail's body out of its spiral shell with its long, thin, curved upper bill.

TURKEY VULTURE
Cathartes aura

The turkey vulture, like all vultures, is a raptor, even though it doesn't kill its own prey. Instead, turkey vultures eat carrion. They find dead animals by soaring and using both their sharp eyesight and sense of smell. Turkey vultures' feet, unlike other raptors' feet, are weak, but their strong, sharp bills are able to slice through tough animal skins.

BURROWING OWL
Athene cunicularia

The burrowing owl lives in tunnels in grasslands and deserts. It eats a lot of insects, but it also catches small mammals, reptiles, frogs, and birds. Burrowing owls store extra prey to tide them over when they're sitting on their eggs or caring for their young. In 1997, scientists found an owl burrow stuffed with more than 200 rodents.

WANDERING ALBATROSS
Diomedea exulans

A wandering albatross soars over oceans on wings that can measure up to 11 feet (3.4 m) from wingtip to wingtip. It feeds mainly on squid and fish. It can smell food floating on the ocean from as far as 12 miles (19.3 km) away.

The bald eagle isn't bald! Its name comes from an old usage of the word "bald" to mean "marked with white." A bald eagle's head and tail turn white when it's about four or five years old.

BALD EAGLE

If you're a fish, the last thing you want to see is a bald eagle plunging toward you—because it may *be* the last thing you see. This giant bird drops from the sky at speeds up to 100 miles an hour (161 km/h). It swoops over the water and seizes its prey with long, sharp talons. The talons sink into the fish. Then the eagle flaps away to land and tears its prey to bits with its strong, hooked beak.

The eagle's black talons get their power from muscles and tough cords, called tendons, in its legs. These tendons have a special structure that helps the eagle "lock" its grip on the fish. That way, the eagle doesn't have to keep squeezing really hard with muscle power alone.

The bald eagle is such a beautiful, powerful bird that in 1782 it was chosen to be the symbol of the United States—though Benjamin Franklin famously joked that it shouldn't be, because an eagle was "too lazy to fish for himself" and steals fish from other raptors. That is only partly true. While bald eagles do hassle other birds to steal their fish, they also work hard to catch their own.

Being the national symbol, however, didn't protect bald eagles from being harmed by people. The birds became an endangered species over time for many reasons. For example, they were shot by farmers and fishers and accidentally poisoned by pesticides.

Fortunately, the U.S. government passed a law in 1940 that helped protect eagles (they could not be hunted without a permit). Then the pesticide DDT was banned in 1972. Today, bald eagles nest again in every state (except Hawaii, where they never lived anyway).

FACTS

FAMILY Accipitridae

OTHER COMMON NAMES American eagle, fishing eagle, white-headed eagle

SCIENTIFIC NAME *Haliaeetus leucocephalus*

SIZE 31 to 37 inches (79 to 94 cm)

FOOD Fish, ducks, geese, small mammals, reptiles, frogs, crabs, carrion

HABITAT Seashores, rivers, lakes, marshes

RANGE North America

Bald eagles build huge nests. Every year, they add more sticks and leaves to the nest. One of the biggest nests ever built was in Florida. It was as tall as a two-story building!

A female harpy eagle carries prey back to her nest to share with her chicks. She has already eaten half of it.

HARPY EAGLE

All raptors have feet for gripping and killing, but the talons of a harpy eagle are especially menacing. Each foot bristles with four talons that are the size of a grizzly bear's claws! The eagle's toes grip with a strength that's powerful enough to crush bones as big as the ones in your arm.

A harpy eagle needs superstrong feet because it hunts fairly large prey. It seizes animals such as monkeys and sloths. Sloths are about the size of a medium-size dog and spend lots of time hanging upside down from tree branches. Imagine getting your dinner by grabbing an animal that is close to your weight or even weighs more than you—with your *feet*—and flying off with it!

Even though a harpy eagle's wings spread up to 6.5 feet (2 m) from tip to tip, they are on the short side for such big birds. That's because harpy eagles don't soar high in the sky to find prey—they hunt in forests and have to dodge branches and trunks as they fly. Their long tails help them steer as they zip through the trees.

Like other eagles, though, this bird has sharp eyesight. A harpy eagle can clearly see something that's just one inch (2 cm) in size from a distance of nearly 660 feet (200 m). If you could do that, you could see what's on a postage stamp that's a city block or two away!

This eagle does a lot of sitting high in a tree as it hunts. It watches and waits for its prey. It listens, too. A harpy eagle has a circle of feathers around its face, much like an owl. The feathers help funnel sound to its ears. This, in turn, helps it hear prey rustling in the dim light of the forest.

FACTS

FAMILY Accipitridae

OTHER COMMON NAMES American harpy eagle, royal hawk

SCIENTIFIC NAME *Harpia harpyja*

SIZE 35 to 41 inches (89 to 105 cm)

FOOD Sloths, monkeys, armadillos, small wild pigs, and other medium-size mammals; parrots and other large birds; iguanas

HABITAT Lowland tropical forests

RANGE Southern Mexico, Central America, South America

Young harpy eagles stay with their parents for about a year before heading off on their own.

119

MARTIAL EAGLE

FACTS

FAMILY Accipitridae

OTHER COMMON NAMES
Martial hawk-eagle

SCIENTIFIC NAME
Polemaetus bellicosus

SIZE 31 to 38 inches (78 to 96 cm)

FOOD Medium-size mammals, birds, and reptiles

HABITAT Open woodlands, savannas, grasslands, thornbush, dry lands

RANGE Sub-Saharan Africa

"Martial" means "warlike," but the martial eagle isn't interested in war. Its fierce attitude and its power are just tools for getting food. For a martial eagle, that food is mostly medium-size animals.

What exactly it eats depends on where it lives in Africa. In some places, there are lots of small antelopes and chunky little rock-dwelling animals called hyraxes—so that's what the eagle eats. In other places, hares or birds make up most of its meals.

A martial eagle looks for prey by soaring high above the ground. When it sees prey, it dives toward it, then smacks into it with its powerful legs. These mighty hunters have even managed to kill jackals and servals (a kind of wildcat). In South Africa's Kruger National Park, many martial eagles like to feast on big lizards called water monitors.

The martial eagle is the largest eagle in Africa and one of the world's biggest. Unfortunately, it's also becoming one of the most threatened. It sometimes kills lambs and goat kids. As a result, eagles are killed by farmers, who shoot or poison them. Habitat loss is also a threat as people turn wild lands into farmland.

What's being done to help martial eagles? Different organizations are using solutions that have helped other kinds of predators in other places. For example, farmers in some parts of Africa are paid for the loss of their sheep and goats that are killed by eagles.

Africa's smallest raptor is the pygmy falcon. It is less than eight inches (20 cm) long.

Martial eagles nest in tall trees, so big poles that hold up power lines look like good nest sites to them. But these electric lines are dangerous and have killed many eagles. In some places, people move the birds' nests to platforms that are safer. Power companies may someday put devices on power structures that will stop eagles from nesting on the dangerous parts.

STELLER'S SEA EAGLE

FACTS

FAMILY Accipitridae

OTHER COMMON NAMES
White-shouldered eagle,
Pacific eagle

SCIENTIFIC NAME
Haliaeetus pelagicus

SIZE 34 to 41 inches (85 to 105 cm)

FOOD Fish, crabs, shellfish,
squid, seabirds, ducks, mammals,
carrion

HABITAT Sea coasts, islands,
large rivers and lakes

RANGE Far eastern Russia,
Japan, China, Korean peninsula

Meet the bald eagle's cousin in Asia. The Steller's sea eagle is like a supersize bald eagle, with white legs and wing patches instead of a white head. On that head is a massive yellow bill that's bigger than its cranium (the part of its skull that holds its eyes and brain).

A sea eagle's huge beak is perfect for the task of tearing apart fish. It starts its fishing expedition by sitting in a tree or on a cliff to look for prey. It may also seek prey by soaring over the water. When it spots a fish, it dives and snatches it in its mighty talons. Sea eagles also stand on the water's edge to fish. They'll eat dead fish they find on shore, too.

This giant eagle breeds along parts of Russia's far eastern coast, where its favorite food is salmon. It feeds heavily on salmon that are swimming upriver to lay eggs in streams. In winter, many Steller's sea eagles migrate south to parts of Japan, South Korea, and China.

These birds are very rare. Scientists estimate there may be as few as 4,600 to 5,100 of them left in the wild. The birds have been affected by logging of forests. They are also harmed by overfishing. That's when the fishing industry takes too many fish from an area so that there are fewer fish left to reproduce. Fish numbers then drop, which means less food for the eagle.

Because of overfishing, sea eagles in Japan have resorted to feeding on the remains of deer left in the forest after people have gone deer hunting. This posed another problem: Hunters used bullets that contained lead, and birds died because they swallowed them. The good news is that this led to a ban on lead bullets, which can only help this beautiful bird survive.

Researchers studying wild eagles found that a Steller's sea eagle can eat nearly two pounds (0.9 kg) of fish in just three to four minutes—probably thanks to its huge, strong bill.

The Steller's sea eagle has an average wingspan of seven feet (2.1 m). Females are larger than males.

Crowned eagles can't always carry off and eat their prey if it's too heavy for them to lift, so they may take prey in pieces and tuck it away into trees to eat later.

CROWNED EAGLE

The crowned eagle isn't as big as Africa's largest eagle, the martial eagle, but it's considered to be the most powerful. That's because this predator often kills prey that can be four times its size. Crowned eagles weigh from 6 to 10 pounds (2.7 to 4.7 kg), but they can kill animals that weigh as much as 44 pounds (20 kg).

A crowned eagle can launch an attack like this thanks to some outsize talons. The rear-facing toe on each of its feet ends in a talon that can be as big as the talons of much larger kinds of eagles. It can use these special talons to break the backbone of its prey. But often it doesn't have to—just a thump from its talons as it hits its prey is often enough to kill it.

Crowned eagles often pick out their prey by perching in a tree near a water hole. When animals come to drink, the eagle pounces. But the crowned eagle's favorite prey is monkeys. It can hunt monkeys in treetops because it's built a lot like the harpy eagle of Central and South America, which also hunts in forests (see p. 118). Like that raptor, it has short, broad wings and a long tail that help it twist and turn among tree trunks and branches.

Sometimes, a female crowned eagle and her mate hunt together. One eagle flies above the trees and calls. This gets the monkeys' attention and causes them to start crying out in alarm, which clues the other eagle in to the monkeys' whereabouts. Then this eagle dives in and grabs a monkey—often by the head.

FACTS

FAMILY Accipitridae

OTHER COMMON NAMES
Crowned hawk-eagle, African crowned eagle

SCIENTIFIC NAME
Stephanoaetus coronatus

SIZE 32 to 36 inches (80 to 90 cm)

FOOD Mammals, especially monkeys

HABITAT Forests, woodlands, savannas, shrublands

RANGE Sub-Saharan Africa

The Verreaux's eagle, along with the crowned eagle and martial eagle, is the third of Africa's "big three" eagles. Its main prey is the rock hyrax, which is a mammal about the size of a big rabbit.

125

PHILIPPINE EAGLE

FACTS

FAMILY Accipitridae

OTHER COMMON NAMES
Monkey-eating eagle, great
Philippine eagle

SCIENTIFIC NAME
Pithecophaga jefferyi

SIZE 35 to 39 inches (90 to 100 cm)

FOOD Monkeys, flying lemurs,
bats, rats, and other mammals;
birds; reptiles

HABITAT Forests

RANGE Four islands in the
Philippines

A female Philippine eagle lays one egg every two years. Both parents care for the young until it can survive on its own.

What's in a name? Sometimes, the wrong information! The Philippine eagle was once called the monkey-eating eagle. That's like people being called "the pizza-eating primate"! It's true that these eagles eat monkeys, but they also eat a wide variety of other prey.

So in 1978, its common name was changed to Philippine eagle in an official proclamation by the president of the Philippines. Later, in 1995, the eagle became the nation's official national bird.

The Philippine eagle hunts in the forest, like a harpy eagle. It may sit and watch for prey or flap from branch to branch. Philippine eagles also hunt in pairs, like crowned eagles do: One eagle attracts the prey's attention, and the other eagle zips in to attack it. These eagles will also stick their talons into holes and niches in trees to snag prey.

This species is one of the world's biggest eagles. It's also the rarest eagle and one of the rarest birds of all. Scientists estimate there may be only about 750 left, or perhaps even as few as 250.

These eagles have become critically endangered because they've lost much of their habitat. Forests have been cut down for logging. Farmers also cut and burn trees to clear land for farming. Sadly, the birds are often shot for no reason at all.

Efforts to help Philippine eagles survive include raising them in captivity. Then young birds can be released into the wild when they're grown up. Laws have been passed to protect their nests and to educate people in the Philippines about these birds.

Philippine eagles can live more than 40 years in captivity. They are thought to live about 20 years in the wild.

A honey buzzard's nostrils are narrow slits, which helps to keep dirt out when it's digging up wasp nests.

HONEY BUZZARD

What kind of a raptor goes around digging up its food like a hungry dog? The honey buzzard—which is actually a kind of raptor called a kite, and not a buzzard.

A honey buzzard leaves all that zipping around in the sky and plunging toward the ground to other raptors. It's not interested in chasing birds, snaring fish, or seizing rabbits. What it wants are the plump, juicy young of wasps, hornets, and bees.

First, the honey buzzard has to find an insect nest. It does this by spotting and then following flying insects. It may possibly use its sense of smell, too. Then the honey buzzard gets to work digging in the soil with its long-toed feet. Unlike other raptors, the honey buzzard's talons aren't extremely hooked. This helps it to dig as well as to walk and run on the ground.

The honey buzzard feasts on grubs (young insects). It calmly plucks grubs out of their little cells in the nest with its slim beak.

Of course, the adult insects buzz furiously around the honey buzzard. But the buzzard is protected from stings by tiny, closely packed feathers on its face. Thick scales protect its feet and legs from stings as well. Some scientists suspect that the honey buzzard's feathers may produce a substance that repels or calms down insects.

Honey buzzards breed in Europe. In early fall, they fly to wintering grounds in Africa. They fly back to Europe at winter's end to feast on the grubs that will hatch in springtime.

FACTS

FAMILY Accipitridae

OTHER COMMON NAMES European honey buzzard, western honey buzzard

SCIENTIFIC NAME *Pernis apivorus*

SIZE 20 to 22 inches (51 to 56 cm)

FOOD Mainly young (larvae and pupae) of wasps and bees; also insects, worms, frogs, salamanders, small reptiles, small mammals, eggs, fruit, berries

HABITAT Open woodlands, forests, lowland rain forests

RANGE Europe, Africa, western Asia

An Asian species called the crested honey buzzard may be the only predator of the Asian giant hornet, which is about two inches (5 cm) long (see pp. 234–235).

PEREGRINE FALCON

FACTS

FAMILY Falconidae

OTHER COMMON NAMES
Duck hawk

SCIENTIFIC NAME
Falco peregrinus

SIZE 14.2 to 19.3 inches
(36 to 49 cm)

FOOD Mainly birds; occasionally
reptiles, insects, and small
mammals

HABITAT Grasslands, seashores,
wetlands, tundras, scrublands,
mountains

RANGE Every continent except
Antarctica, also oceanic islands

A peregrine
falcon's nostrils have
tiny structures in them
that break up the air flowing
in as it stoops. This
adaptation lets it breathe
normally even as
air rushes in at
high speed.

Zoom! **A peregrine falcon dives headfirst from** the sky. It rockets toward its prey, a pigeon, at more than 200 miles an hour (320 km/h). That's about as fast as a race car.

The pigeon doesn't stand a chance. It's stabbed by the falcon's extra-long hind talon, seized by its strong toes, and bitten in the neck. Then the falcon carries its prey to a perch to eat it or starts tearing it apart and feeding while still in flight.

The peregrine falcon's spectacular dive is called a stoop. It stoops at amazing speeds because it starts from very high in the sky. As it stoops, it tucks its wings close to its body and folds its tail. It turns into a feathered missile that dashes easily through the air. A protective, clear eyelid slips across each eye so it can still see without the risk of dust damaging its eyes.

A peregrine falcon can also fly fast by flapping without stooping. In this way, it can chase prey at speeds up to 69 miles an hour (112 km/h). Its long, slim wings also help it twist and turn quickly to keep up with equally fast-flying prey.

Peregrine falcons also hunt by perching on cliffs and watching for their next meal. At sea, they've been known to perch on ships. On the ground, peregrines will walk to find insects and other small land-based prey to eat.

These birds also nest on cliff ledges. They don't build nests. Instead, they just scrape out a little dip in the dirt or gravel on a ledge. Then they lay their eggs in this dip. Today, peregrine falcons often nest in cities on skyscrapers and bridges, which are like cliffs to them. They find plenty of pigeons to eat!

Peregrine falcons that breed in the Arctic migrate south in winter to the southern tip of South America. They might make round-trip journeys of 15,500 miles (25,000 km) in a year.

OSPREY

FACTS

FAMILY Pandionidae

OTHER COMMON NAMES
Fish hawk, fish eagle, sea hawk

SCIENTIFIC NAME
Pandion haliaetus

SIZE 21 to 23 inches (54 to 58 cm)

FOOD Fish; rarely, birds, reptiles, and small mammals

HABITAT Seashores, lakes, rivers, bays, marshes, estuaries, ponds, and other shallow waters

RANGE All continents except Antarctica

Ospreys will eagerly build nests on human-made nesting platforms. These platforms are a big help to ospreys in places where waterside forests have been cut down.

A slippery, slimy fish is hard to hold. The slime that helps it glide through water and protects its skin can also help it slip from the grip of a predator. But it would take an awful lot of slime for a fish to escape the clutches of an osprey.

An osprey flies over the water to look for fish. It drops down feetfirst when it spots one and plunges into the water at speeds up to 40 miles an hour (64 km/h). Then it sinks its talons into the fish. Spikes on the soles of the osprey's feet give it extra grip on its wriggling prey.

Finally, the osprey secures its grip even more by turning an outer toe on each foot backward. This trick lets an osprey's foot grip a fish with two toes on each side instead of three on one side and one on the other, like an eagle does. This setup makes it less likely that the fish will get away by twisting its body back and forth. Owls are the only other raptors that can turn their toes this way.

A male osprey has a unique way of attracting a female. He zooms high in the air and then swoops down while calling loudly. Up and down and up again he goes, with his legs hanging down and talons clutching a fish or nesting material. This display is called a sky-dance.

Like eagles and peregrine falcons, ospreys suffered from the effects of the pesticide DDT building up in their bodies in the mid-1900s. (A pesticide is a substance that kills insects.) The ospreys laid eggs with thin shells that were crushed before chicks hatched. Osprey numbers climbed again after DDT was banned in 1972.

However, new chemicals are invented all the time, and some of them are harmful to wildlife and people, too. Scientists study ospreys and measure substances in their blood and eggs to find out about chemicals that are dangerous in the environment.

An osprey turns the fish it catches so that its head points forward. This makes the fish less of an obstacle to the wind and helps the osprey fly more easily while carrying its load.

A secretary bird can walk from 12 to 18 miles (20 to 30 km) in a day as it looks for food.

SECRETARY BIRD

The secretary bird struts across open spaces as if it knows it's a one-of-a-kind raptor. With its long legs, it looks more like a cousin of the stork instead of a hawk. But it's truly a raptor, and like other raptors it kills with its feet.

A secretary bird stamps its feet near shrubs or bunches of grass to scare small animals out of hiding. It can also run fast, so it chases prey, too. It snaps up small prey with its beak. It attacks larger prey by kicking it to knock it down and stamping on it. Scientists have measured the strength of a secretary bird's kick and found that it's about equal to a force five times the bird's weight.

With a kick like that, no wonder a secretary bird isn't afraid of attacking snakes—even venomous ones. A secretary bird that meets a snake kicks and stomps on it. It also stabs it with the sharp hind claw of its foot. The snake tries to bite the secretary bird, but the bird's legs are armored with heavy scales. The bird also flails its big wings to ward off the snake's lunges.

A fire sweeping across the plains is bad news for most animals, but it's a dinner bell for secretary birds. They know that fire drives a lot of small animals out into the open.

A secretary bird never sits at a desk or writes, so how did it get its name? One story claims that people thought the birds looked like old-fashioned clerks, or secretaries, from the 1800s. These secretaries were men who wore wigs, like many men of that time, and often stuck their pens in their wigs when they weren't using them. The quills on the birds' heads reminded people of these pens.

FACTS

FAMILY Sagittariidae

OTHER COMMON NAMES None

SCIENTIFIC NAME
Sagittarius serpentarius

SIZE 4 to 5 feet (1.2 to 1.5 m)

FOOD Small mammals, young birds, reptiles, amphibians, insects, eggs

HABITAT Grasslands, savannas, scrublands

RANGE Sub-Saharan Africa

The caracara of Central and South America is a raptor that hunts on the ground in grasslands like a secretary bird, though it grabs its prey instead of stamping on and kicking it.

SNOWY OWL

FACTS

FAMILY Strigidae

OTHER COMMON NAMES
Arctic owl, white owl

SCIENTIFIC NAME
Bubo scandiacus

SIZE 20.5 to 28 inches
(52 to 71 cm)

FOOD Rodents, rabbits, birds,
fish, carrion

HABITAT Tundras, prairies,
beaches, marshes

RANGE Northern North America,
Greenland, northern Eurasia

A male snowy owl turns whiter and whiter as it gets older and may even turn pure white. A female snowy owl remains marked with some dark spots and streaks.

The snowy owl's name and its white feathers tell you where you're likely to find it. This owl breeds on the tundra of Earth's far north, or Arctic, region. The tundra is a vast, treeless land that is chilly in summer and extremely cold in winter.

Snow covers the tundra for large parts of the year, but the snowy owl is adapted to this harsh climate. Its white coloring camouflages it in snow. Thick feathers keep it warm. Fluffy feathers cover its nostrils. Even its legs and feet are feathered. It breeds on the tundra in the short summertime, when wildflowers bloom and bogs and ponds form.

Unlike most owls, the snowy owl usually hunts by day. But like all owls, it has sharp eyes and keen hearing. It can spot prey from far away and even hear it creeping beneath the snow. It usually hunts by sitting, watching, waiting, and then flying when prey is in sight. It's a raptor, so that prey is grabbed and killed by its sharp talons and then torn apart by its hooked beak.

The snowy owl's favorite food is a chunky rodent called a lemming. An adult owl might eat three or more lemmings each day. In the breeding season, the male may dangle a lemming from his beak or talons as he courts a female. Then he brings tidbits to the female as she sits on her eggs. When the chicks hatch, Dad keeps fetching food and Mom feeds it to them. Dinner is usually—you guessed it—lemmings!

Sometimes, lemming populations drop, and the owls may not nest or raise young that year because food is hard to find. Lack of food may also cause some snowy owls to fly south in winter. Then these birds pop up in places such as Texas and Florida.

A snowy owl might eat more than 1,600 lemmings in one year.

A great horned owl will stash extra prey to eat later. In the Arctic, this stored prey may freeze. In that case, the owl sits on it. This warms the frozen food so that it thaws out and can be eaten.

GREAT HORNED OWL

Being as quiet as a mouse won't help a mouse that's anywhere near a great horned owl. The owl can hear a mouse's squeaks from up to 900 feet (275 m) away. The feathers on its face, which funnel sounds to its ears, help its sharp hearing.

Those ears are hidden from sight—they are *not* the things sticking up from its head. These "horns" are just tufts of feathers, called plumicorns. Scientists have bounced around ideas about why some owls have plumicorns, but so far nobody knows for sure how the owls use them.

Good hearing is important for the owl, because it usually hunts at night. A hungry owl begins its hunt by perching, watching, and listening. It tilts its head to hone in on its prey and then swoops. The unlucky prey never hears the owl approaching because its flight is silent: Its wings are fringed with special feathers that muffle the sound of air rushing by. Velvety feathers on its wings and body also help absorb sound.

Prey is caught with the owl's strong toes and talons. Its grip is so strong that its feet can cut through the spine of larger prey such as raccoons. Small prey, such as a mouse, is swallowed whole, while larger prey is carried off to a safe spot for eating. The owl rests on a branch after its meal. Its body will digest the prey's flesh, but fur, claws, teeth, bones, and other bits form pellets that the owl will regurgitate, or throw up.

Great horned owls are big and strong enough to tackle animals larger than they are. They've been known to attack other predatory birds, such as hawks and peregrine falcons. Great horned owls even attack animals with strong defenses, such as prickly porcupines.

FACTS

FAMILY Strigidae

OTHER COMMON NAMES Tiger owl, hoot owl, skunk owl, cat owl, king owl, eagle owl

SCIENTIFIC NAME *Bubo virginianus*

SIZE 18 to 25 inches (46 to 63 cm)

FOOD Mammals, birds, lizards, snakes, frogs, insects, scorpions

HABITAT Deserts, edges of tundras, wetlands, woods, forests, rain forests, grasslands, farmlands, backyards, parks, cities

RANGE North America, Central America, parts of South America

Great horned owls are one of the only predators that regularly catch and eat skunks. This habit earned the great horned owl its nickname of "skunk owl," and it often smells just as bad as its stinky meal!

GREAT SKUA

FACTS

FAMILY Stercorariidae

OTHER COMMON NAMES
Bonxie, skua gull, sea hawk, sea hen

SCIENTIFIC NAME
Stercorarius skua

SIZE 21 to 24 inches (53 to 61 cm)

FOOD Fish, birds, small mammals, insects, eggs, carrion

HABITAT Oceans, islands

RANGE North Atlantic

Great skuas nest on coasts. Chicks leave the nest when they're about seven weeks old. As adults, most chicks will nest in the same areas where they were hatched.

This bird looks a lot like just another gull— a gull with rather untidy brown feathers. But the great skua is actually such a strong, fierce predator that it is often called "the pirate of the skies."

At sea, a skua feeds on fish. It catches fish by flying low over the ocean's surface or while swimming and snapping them up with its beak. It also bullies other seabirds into giving up their meals. It will chase and dive-bomb these birds until they drop their prey. Then it grabs the food in midair.

A seabird pestered by a skua may be so desperate to get away that it will even throw up food from its stomach. The skua has no problem scarfing up this yucky meal.

A skua isn't a much better neighbor on land. Skuas nest mainly on the Faroe Islands in the North Atlantic as well as on islands around Norway, Iceland, and Scotland. They are often found near colonies of gulls and other seabirds. The skuas visit these colonies to feed on eggs and chicks.

Meanwhile, a pair of skuas raises its own young in a shallow nest on flat ground. The nest is little more than a small dip filled with bits of grass and moss. The male and female take turns incubating the eggs and then feeding the chicks. If anything comes near, the skuas will fiercely protect their young. They'll raise their big wings and screech warnings. They'll also take to the air to dive and scream at the intruder.

When breeding season is over, great skuas head out to the open ocean. They spend these months offshore.

Many skuas migrate south to feed off the coasts of southern Europe and Africa. Others wander toward Canada and New England in the United States. Here a great skua is flying with a dead arctic tern.

141

Southern giant petrels can be either white with a few black feathers, or brown with some white feathers.

SOUTHERN GIANT PETREL

Why are southern giant petrels known as

stinkpots? You would quickly find out if you went too close to a petrel nest. Petrels have a very smelly self-defense system!

Part of a petrel's stomach stores up a supply of oil made from fats and other substances from its meals. The stored-up oil is filled with energy that can help a petrel go for a long time between meals. It can also help a petrel chick survive while its parents are off fetching food at sea. For an adult petrel, a good supply of oil is like traveling with a full tank of gas.

But the oil comes in handy if the bird is threatened, too, because it can squirt the stinky oil out of its beak at its attacker! It can spray the oil as far as three feet (1 m). The smell is bad enough that it is hard to get rid of—people who've been "slimed" by the birds say the smell lingers in their clothes for years.

If the attacker is another seabird, the oil can also be deadly. It coats feathers and destroys their ability to lock together. Feathers keep a bird warm and waterproof, so you can see how spoiled feathers would spell doom for a seabird.

Giant petrels are both hunters and scavengers. As hunters, they catch fish and squid near the ocean's surface and prey on penguin chicks and other small birds on land. Their sharply hooked bills are also useful tools for scavenging because they can easily tear open dead whales and seals.

Fishing vessels that use long lines with lots of hooks on them often kill petrels and other seabirds. Birds and other animals accidentally killed in this way are called bycatch. Efforts to reduce bycatch include weights on the line so the hooks are quickly dunked underwater before birds can get at them.

FACTS

FAMILY Procellariidae

OTHER COMMON NAMES
Stinker, stinkpot, nelly, glutton, sea vulture, giant fulmar

SCIENTIFIC NAME
Macronectes giganteus

SIZE 34 to 39 inches (85 to 100 cm)

FOOD Fish, squid, octopuses, krill, birds, carrion

HABITAT Rocky shores, open oceans

RANGE Antarctic and subantarctic region

Seabirds take in a lot of salt water with their food. Salt builds up in their blood and needs to be washed out. In a petrel, the tube on top of its bill drains this salty liquid.

SHOEBILL

FACTS

FAMILY Balaenicipitidae

OTHER COMMON NAMES
Whale-headed stork, whalehead, shoe-billed stork

SCIENTIFIC NAME
Balaeniceps rex

SIZE 43 to 55 inches (110 to 140 cm)

FOOD Fish, frogs, turtles, reptiles, carrion

HABITAT Swamps, marshes

RANGE Eastern central Africa

A shoebill stork tucks in its head when it flies. Its powerful wings stretch about 7.7 feet (2.3 m) from tip to tip.

Having a beak that looks like a big wooden Dutch shoe doesn't sound like an excellent feature for a predator—unless, of course, you're a shoebill. A shoebill's one-of-a-kind bill is adapted for the job of grabbing, holding, and swallowing big, slippery fish.

A shoebill hunts mainly by standing stock-still in a marsh or swamp. Its favorite kind of wetland has shallow water. That's where it can most easily catch its favorite prey, the lungfish. Unlike most fish, a lungfish can get oxygen by breathing air. In shallow water, it tends to come to the surface often to take a breath, which puts it in striking range of the shoebill.

A shoebill may freeze like a statue for up to half an hour waiting for a fish to appear. When it sees its prey, it lunges forward with its bill open wide. Flapping its big wings, it stands up straight again. It swings its head to shake out any water plants and other pieces of debris that came in with the fish. It may also cut off its prey's head with the sharp edges of its beak.

After catching and eating a fish, the shoebill walks to a new spot to hunt. It has very long toes that help spread its weight and make it easier to walk on soggy ground and water plants.

Shoebills live and hunt alone most of the time. They pair up in breeding season. Their nest is a big pile of water plants. It may be built on an island or float on the water. The female bird can lay up to three eggs, but usually only one chick survives after hatching. What happens to the others? Sometimes they're eaten by predators. Sometimes they starve because the biggest, oldest chick hogs all the food. Other times, they die as a result of pecking by that biggest chick.

A shoebill's beak can be up to 12 inches (25 cm) long and 5 inches (13 cm) wide. This one is gulping down a lungfish in a swamp in Uganda.

The black heron's wings are adapted for this kind of fishing, which is called canopy feeding. Its flight feathers are especially wide, which helps it make a lightproof shade.

BLACK HERON

Like other kinds of herons, the black heron has long legs, a long neck, and a long bill. Like many herons, too, it likes to eat fish. But the black heron has a special trick it uses when it hunts. It turns into a walking umbrella—the better to both find and fool its prey.

The black heron steps carefully in the water with its big, yellow feet. As it gets near a fish, it suddenly snaps its wings forward. The wings form a big, bowl-shaped umbrella over the water. It shades the water, which may help the heron see better, just as you might shield your eyes in bright sunlight (though many researchers point out that the heron will make an umbrella even on a cloudy day).

Shady spots also attract fish, because they're usually a good place to hide. That is, if the shady spot isn't a hungry heron. The heron keeps its head under its wings to see where the fish is. It may stir the water with a foot to lure fish, too. If it spots prey, it grabs it with its bill. Then the heron folds up its wings and moves on to try the trick in another spot.

This heron also has plumes sticking out of its head and neck that close off the top of the umbrella and make it dark underneath.

FACTS

FAMILY Ardeidae

OTHER COMMON NAMES Black egret, umbrella bird

SCIENTIFIC NAME *Egretta ardesiaca*

SIZE 17 to 26 inches (43 to 66 cm)

FOOD Fish, amphibians, crustaceans, insects

HABITAT Shallow lakes, ponds, marshes, riverside areas, mangrove forest edges, tidal rivers, rice fields, seasonally flooded grasslands

RANGE Sub-Saharan Africa, Madagascar

Sometimes a lot of black herons feed in the same spot. They're not working together, though—they're just sharing the space.

ANHINGA

FACTS

FAMILY Anhingidae

OTHER COMMON NAMES
Water turkey, snakebird, darter

SCIENTIFIC NAME
Anhinga anhinga

SIZE 30 to 37 inches (75 to 95 cm)

FOOD Fish, water snakes, frogs, crustaceans, insects

HABITAT Swamps, marshes, bays, lakes, lagoons, rivers

RANGE Southeastern United States, Mexico, Panama, Cuba, Central America, South America

The name "anhinga" comes from the language of the Tupi people of Brazil and means "devil bird."

An anhinga swimming underwater looks like a strange blend of a turkey, a duck, and a snake. Its large, wide tail fans open like a Thanksgiving turkey's tail. Its big, webbed yellow feet paddle like a duck's.

As for the snake, that's the bird's neck and head! The anhinga has a long, slender neck and head, which it sticks into nooks and crannies underwater in search of fish. It often swims with just its head and neck showing above the water, which makes it look even more like a snake.

The anhinga is adapted so that it doesn't bob around on the top of the water like a cork. It has heavy, dense bones to help it dive and swim close to the bottom of shallow waters to hunt. Its feathers aren't waterproof, like a duck's or goose's feathers. Instead, they get wet, which also helps the bird sink. An anhinga can also control the amount of air in its body to help it rise or fall in the water.

When the anhinga finds a fish, it stabs with its long, sharp, pointy bill and spears it. This lightning-fast jab is possible thanks to the way its neck is hinged about halfway down its length.

Then the anhinga rises to the surface to eat its fish. Its bill has jagged edges like those of a bread knife to help it hold on to its slippery prey. It has to juggle the fish to get it off its bill so it can swallow it headfirst. The anhinga may fling the fish into the air and catch it with its bill open wide or swim to shore to rub the fish off its bill.

If it's done hunting, the anhinga flaps to a perch. Then it holds out its wings to warm up in the sunlight.

An anhinga does not have open nostrils on the outside of its bill. Air has to enter its bill through its mouth. This adaptation helps the bird avoid getting water up its nose.

Shrikes impale their prey on the spikes of barbed-wire fences as well as on thorns. They also stuff prey into small spaces, such as cracks in bark.

NORTHERN SHRIKE

A northern shrike is a songbird with a sharp, hooked bill a bit like a hawk's. It begins its hunt by sitting on a branch, pole, or other perch out in the open to look for prey. If it spots a flying insect, it darts into the air and zooms to catch it with its bill. It may eat the bug in midair if it's very hungry. A shrike also goes after small birds in flight. It forces a bird out of the air by striking it with its bill or grabbing it with its claws and plummeting with it to the ground. To catch mice, voles, and other small ground animals, a shrike zips toward its prey and then drops down to catch it.

A shrike's hooked bill, so useful for tearing apart prey, is also adapted for killing. It can kill prey by knocking it hard in the back of the head with its beak. It can also cut through the necks of animals with backbones. The edge of its upper bill has a pair of sharp, toothlike points that it uses to bite the necks of birds, rodents, and reptiles.

The shrike has another habit that adds to its fame as a fierce hunter: It jams prey into notches of trees and also stabs its victims onto spines, thorns, or other sharp objects. Skewering its food helps the little bird tug at it and rip it apart to eat it. It's also a good way to store extra prey to eat at a later time.

Northern shrikes also prepare some foods in particular ways. They'll impale certain kinds of grasshoppers on spikes, wait a few days, and then just eat the heads and abdomens—discarding the poisonous middle section.

FACTS

FAMILY Laniidae

OTHER COMMON NAMES Great gray shrike, butcherbird, nine-killer, winter shrike

SCIENTIFIC NAME *Lanius excubitor*

SIZE 9.1 to 9.4 inches (23 to 24 cm)

FOOD Insects, spiders, small mammals, birds, small reptiles, frogs

HABITAT Evergreen forests in the far north (taiga), wetlands, forest edges, grasslands, fields with scattered trees and shrubs

RANGE North America, northern Eurasia, northern Africa, India, China, Japan

The northern shrike is so determined to keep intruders out of its hunting territory that it will even attack golden eagles, owls, and hawks that trespass.

COILS, FANGS & VICIOUS VENOM

A white-footed mouse makes a meal for a black timber rattlesnake.

ALL ABOUT PREDATORY REPTILES & AMPHIBIANS

Reptiles and amphibians are cold-blooded animals, which means their body temperatures change according to the temperature around them. Their bodies do not generate a lot of heat the way a mammal's or a bird's body does.

These animals have many ways of changing their body temperature. If they're cold, for example, they can sit in sunlight to warm up. That's why scientists use the term "ectotherm" instead of "cold-blooded." "Ectotherm" means "outside heat" and refers to how reptiles and amphibians control their body temperature.

Along with the similarities between reptiles and amphibians, there are differences. Reptiles have scaly skin and can lay eggs on land, even in hot, dry places. Amphibians don't have scaly skin and need to lay eggs in water or damp places. Animals such as lizards, snakes, and turtles are reptiles. Amphibians include frogs, toads, and salamanders.

Are they predators or plant-eaters? That depends on the species: Many reptiles are fruit- and leaf-eaters. Take one look at an alligator's mouthful of sharp teeth, however, and you know it's a predator! The reptile world boasts many powerful predators that can tackle prey as large as full-grown cattle. Most predatory reptiles, however, go after smaller prey, such as mice and insects.

Amphibians feed on plants as well as animals as youngsters, but most grow up to eat only meat. Amphibians typically eat lots of small prey, such as insects.

LEATHERBACK TURTLE
Dermochelys coriacea

The biggest species of sea turtle, the leatherback, can grow as long as a big sofa and weigh as much as a cow. It grows to its huge size by eating jellyfish. The leatherback's mouth is adapted for catching this gooey prey. Its jaws have sharp edges for snagging them. Sharp spines that point backward fill its mouth and throat to keep jellyfish from escaping.

WESTERN DIAMONDBACK RATTLESNAKE
Crotalus atrox

Some snakes kill their prey with a bite that injects a dose of a deadly substance called venom. The snake waits until the venom kills its prey and then swallows it whole. A rattlesnake, for example, is venomous. It may slither around to search for prey or sit and wait for prey to wander near it.

CHINESE GIANT SALAMANDER
Andrias davidianus

The Chinese giant salamander is the largest amphibian. It can grow to be 5.9 feet (1.8 m) long, making it larger than most people are tall. It lives in water and feeds at night on fish, frogs, crabs, shrimps, insects, and worms. It is sluggish but can snap quickly to grab prey with its large jaws and then swiftly slurp the prey into its big mouth.

ALLIGATOR SNAPPING TURTLE
Macrochelys temminckii

The alligator snapping turtle dangles a wormlike bit of flesh on its tongue to lure fish right into its jaws. Its sharply hooked jaws are so strong, they can snap a broom handle in two with one bite. It feeds mainly on fish, but it will also eat ducklings and small mammals.

GLOBE-HORNED CHAMELEON
Calumma globifer

A chameleon hunts by standing as still as a stone, swiveling its eyes to look for prey. Its two eyes snap forward when the chameleon spots prey. Then it shoots out its incredibly long and sticky tongue. The tongue tip smacks into the prey, and it is quickly hauled back into the chameleon's mouth.

SALTWATER CROCODILE

What does the world's biggest reptile eat? Anything it can sink its teeth into! The saltwater crocodile is the largest living reptile and, in fact, has remained largely unchanged for 100 million years. A big male can be 23 feet (7 m) long and weigh 2,200 pounds (1,000 kg). That's about as much as three horses ... which this crocodile would gladly eat.

Insects, crabs, and shrimps are what usually fill the bellies of saltwater crocs. Mammals and birds are added to the menu as a croc gets older and bigger. A fully grown saltwater crocodile can tackle anything from fish, sea turtles, dogs, and pigs to formidable animals such as water buffalo and even sharks.

The saltwater crocodile uses two main strategies to hunt its prey. It may swim slowly, looking for prey to seize. More often, it just floats quietly near the water's edge with only its eyes and nostrils showing. Then, when an animal comes down to the shore, the crocodile leaps. It swings its massive tail to push itself out of the water. Then the croc seizes the unlucky animal and drags it into the water, where it drowns.

But even a mighty predator like a saltwater croc starts out small and can be prey itself. First, however, an animal must get past Mom. A female croc guards her nest to keep away animals such as lizards, snakes, rats, and wild pigs that would like to sneak past her and eat her eggs. She also digs up the nest when the young crocs hatch and carries them to the water in her mouth. Yet only about one out of every hundred hatchlings will survive to adulthood. Many of them will actually be killed and eaten by male saltwater crocodiles guarding their territories.

FACTS

FAMILY Crocodylidae

OTHER COMMON NAMES
Estuarine crocodile, Indo-Pacific crocodile, naked-neck crocodile, saltie

SCIENTIFIC NAME
Crocodylus porosus

SIZE 16 to 23 feet (5 to 7 m)

FOOD Insects, amphibians, crustaceans, fish, reptiles, birds, mammals

HABITAT Coastal rivers, lakes, swamps, lagoons, estuaries

RANGE South and Southeast Asia, southwestern Pacific, northern Australia

These saltie crocodiles are able to live in salt water or water that is "brackish"— a mixture of seawater and freshwater.

BLACK CAIMAN

FACTS

FAMILY Alligatoridae

OTHER COMMON NAME
Jacare-assu

SCIENTIFIC NAME
Melanosuchus niger

SIZE 13 to 20 feet (4 to 6 m)

FOOD Mollusks, fish, frogs,
reptiles, birds, mammals

HABITAT Freshwater rivers,
lakes, swamps, streams,
wetlands

RANGE Northern South
America

Lurking in the waters of the Amazon River Basin is a creature with ancestors that lived millions of years ago. It's the black caiman, the largest species in the alligator family and also the biggest predator in its environment.

Like other big reptiles, black caimans start out as easy prey for other animals. Rodents, birds, and raccoonlike animals called coatis all snack on caiman hatchlings. The hatchlings that survive to adulthood, however, do not have to worry about predators anymore. Once a black caiman is a big, powerful adult, it will be avoided even by green anacondas (snakes that can be almost as long as a school bus).

Though a black caiman is big enough to catch large prey, one of its most important foods is fish. It feasts on catfish and sharp-toothed fish called piranhas, as well as other species. It munches on shellfish, too. It also eats a lot of capybaras, which are rodents that look a bit like dog-size guinea pigs. A caiman will also readily catch smaller rodents and other mammals, as well as frogs, reptiles, and birds.

The black caiman's hunting tactics include trapping prey that is swimming near shore—the caiman swims toward the prey so that the shore blocks its escape. The caiman also floats with its head stuck underwater to look for food. If it lunges at fish or other prey, it can leap partly out of the water as it charges.

The black caiman is named for its dark skin, which helps camouflage it and also may help its body soak up heat. (Like all reptiles, a caiman's body temperature is heavily dependent on the temperature of the air around it.)

Young black caimans aren't big enough to hunt fish and mammals. They eat mainly insects, spiders, snails, and crustaceans such as shrimps and crabs.

Black caimans were once heavily hunted for their skins. They nearly went extinct. Today they are protected by law in most countries where they live, and their populations are growing.

A Komodo dragon looks bulky, but it can put on a burst of speed and sprint at about 13 miles an hour (20 km/h).

KOMODO DRAGON

The world's largest lizard, the Komodo dragon, hunts by positioning itself along a trail used by wildlife and remaining motionless until a deer, a pig, or any other animal passes close to it.

Then the dragon leaps into action. If the animal is a rodent or other small prey, the dragon just grabs it and gobbles it down. Larger prey is knocked down first. The dragon slams into the big animal's legs and then slashes it with hooked claws. It also bites and rips with its teeth, which are like steak knives.

The dragon eats nearly every bit of its prey, including hooves, bones, and leathery skin. It's able to gulp down meat at a rate of 5.5 pounds (2.5 kg) a minute! A dragon's stomach is also super stretchy, which lets it eat an incredible 80 percent of its body weight in just one meal.

If the prey manages to survive this attack and stagger away, it's not likely to last long. A Komodo dragon has glands in its jaw that inject venom into the prey's bloodstream. This venom prevents blood from clotting. As a result, the bitten animal will bleed to death. In addition, a dragon's mouth is filled with bacteria, and so are water holes on the islands. An injured animal might end up with a bacterial infection that weakens it or kills it.

For the dragon, a predatory attack isn't always necessary. Komodo dragons aren't fussy eaters; they'll gladly eat carrion. A dragon can smell a dead animal from a distance of 2.5 miles (4 km).

FACTS

FAMILY Varanidae

OTHER COMMON NAMES Komodo monitor, land crocodile

SCIENTIFIC NAME *Varanus komodoensis*

SIZE 8 to 10 feet (2.5 to 3 m)

FOOD Rodents, birds, lizards, deer and other large mammals, carrion

HABITAT Woodlands, savannas

RANGE Indonesian islands of Komodo, Gili Motang, and Flores

Komodo dragons will kill and eat other Komodo dragons, especially hatchlings. That's why newly hatched dragons dart up into trees and live there until they're about four years old. Then they are big enough to defend themselves.

NILE MONITOR

FACTS

FAMILY Varanidae

OTHER COMMON NAMES
Water leguaan

SCIENTIFIC NAME
Varanus niloticus

SIZE Up to 8 feet (2.4 m)

FOOD Rodents, birds, reptiles, fish, frogs, toads, insects, crabs, spiders, millipedes, worms, slugs, eggs, carrion

HABITAT Rivers, lakes, swamps, mangrove forests, woodlands and savannas near water

RANGE Sub-Saharan Africa

The Nile monitor is a cousin of the world's biggest lizard, the Komodo dragon (pp. 160–161). It can grow to nearly the length of a Komodo dragon, which makes it the largest lizard in Africa. Unlike the dragon, however, the Nile monitor is lean and limber. It can swiftly climb trees even as an adult. But it's most at home in and around water. Its adaptations for a watery life include a tail that's flattened from top to bottom, which helps the monitor swim. Its nostrils are located high up on its nose, which is a useful place to have your nostrils if you're swimming just under the water's surface.

This nimble predator hunts for food while flicking its blue forked tongue. Snakes and other prey with bones are killed with a strong bite and tearing claws. A Nile monitor can also easily eat crabs, snails, and other animals with shells. The shape of its skull and jaws helps it exert a crushing force to break the shells open.

Amazingly, a Nile monitor's teeth change over time to help it eat slow-moving, hard-shelled prey. As a hatchling, its teeth are sharp and pointy—just right for seizing skittery insects and quick lizards. Over time, the teeth wear down and become sturdy, blunt pegs that are lined with ridges. Teeth like this allow the monitor to crunch open shells.

A female Nile monitor can dig nests, but she will lay her eggs in termite mounds if she can. She digs into the nest, lays as many as 60 eggs, and walks off. The termites furiously repair the nest. As a result, the eggs are sealed inside a nest where they will stay warm and dry until hatching.

Nile monitors are sometimes eaten by Nile crocodiles—and the monitors often eat the crocodiles' eggs and young. Monitors have been observed hunting as a team to attack a nest and distract the mother crocodile from attacking them.

A Nile monitor in Botswana, Africa, carries a snake it has just killed.

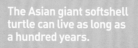

The Asian giant softshell turtle can live as long as a hundred years.

ASIAN GIANT SOFTSHELL TURTLE

The Asian giant softshell turtle is one of the world's largest freshwater turtles. You could also say it's one of the oddest. On most turtles, you can see tough plates that form a shell. Softshell turtles, as their name suggests, have rubbery or leathery shells instead.

An Asian giant softshell turtle has wide, strong flippers for digging into sand. Sticking out of its shell is a very tiny head with a little piglike snout. This head doesn't protrude from under a ledge formed by the shell, like the head of a box turtle does. Instead, its rumpled-looking neck merges with the skin that covers the shell.

Like many turtles, the giant softshell is a sit-and-wait ambush predator. It spends about 95 percent of its life sitting without moving while buried in sand underwater. Only its snout and little eyes stick up from the sand. The turtle may come to the water's surface just twice a day to breathe air, though it can also absorb oxygen from the water through the skin in its mouth and throat.

It stays put until prey swims by. Then its neck and head suddenly stretch out as it strikes like a snake. *Chomp!* It grabs its prey and gulps it down. Then it returns to its motionless ways.

The giant softshell is also rare and endangered. It has long been hunted by people for use as food. Many giant softshells also die as a result of getting caught in fishing nets. Habitat loss along rivers and coasts has also endangered this species. Efforts to help it survive include raising hatchlings in captivity and setting them free in places where there is still habitat for turtles.

FACTS

FAMILY Trionychidae

OTHER COMMON NAMES Cantor's giant softshell turtle, frog-faced softshell turtle

SCIENTIFIC NAME *Pelochelys cantorii*

SIZE 2 feet (0.6 m)

FOOD Fish, crabs, prawns, mollusks, plants

HABITAT Deltas, rivers, estuaries, seacoasts

RANGE India, China, Southeast Asia

A female of this species may leave the water only once a year to lay her eggs on land. She can lay up to 70 eggs at one time.

BLACK MAMBA

FACTS

FAMILY Elapidae

OTHER COMMON NAMES None

SCIENTIFIC NAME
Dendroaspis polylepis

SIZE 8.2 to 14 feet (2.5 to 4.3 m)

FOOD Small rodents, birds

HABITAT Savannas, woodlands, riverside forests, rocky hills

RANGE Sub-Saharan Africa

Africa is home to three other species of mamba. Each species is green, lives in trees, and is smaller than the black mamba, but all are highly venomous.

The black mamba is widely considered to be the most feared snake in Africa—and not by its prey. People are terrified of its deadly bite. The mamba's venom is so strong that a deep bite could kill a person in about 20 minutes. Even hatchlings have fully functioning venom glands and are dangerous right from the time they wriggle out of their shells.

Luckily for humans, they can be saved if bitten by a mamba. A doctor can use a medicine called antivenom to stop the venom's effects if it's given very soon after the snake bites.

It's a different story for a rodent bitten by a black mamba. A mamba kills prey by biting it and then waiting for its deadly venom to kill it. Once the prey is dead, the mamba swallows it whole.

Mambas have another trait that makes them frightening to people: They are one of the fastest snakes in the world. A black mamba can hit speeds of up to 12.5 miles an hour (20 km/h). However, a mamba doesn't zip along at this speed to chase prey or people. It moves this fast to get *away* from danger. It doesn't have any reason to attack people since it doesn't eat them—it only wants to run away and hide.

But if a black mamba can't get away, it will use a behavior that's called a threat display. First, it raises its body so that its head is up high—as much as four feet (1.2 m) off the ground. As if that's not scary enough, the mamba will then spread a thin hood at the back of its neck to look even bigger. It also hisses while opening its mouth wide to reveal its startling black lining. Its mouth's black interior is what gives this snake its name.

A black mamba can grow from being just 15 to 24 inches (38 to 61 cm) at hatching to a length of six feet (1.8 m) by the time it is one year old.

The venom in just one bite of the inland taipan is enough to kill 125,000 mice. It is 740 times as poisonous as the venom of a western diamondback rattlesnake.

INLAND TAIPAN

Australia is home to many species of venomous snakes. One of these snakes is the inland taipan, a snake that lives in remote, dry lands. Its venom is stronger than that of any other snake.

This snake's world is a desert that is sometimes flooded by rain. Here, the soil is thick and claylike. When it dries out, deep cracks form in it. These cracks are great places to hide if you're a snake. The inland taipan slithers into them to get out of blistering heat during the hottest part of the day.

The cracks are also great hiding spots for rats and mice, which are the taipan's main prey. A taipan hunts by day while its prey is sleeping, usually in the morning before temperatures rise. It slips into cracks until it finds a meal. Then it strikes its prey several times, very quickly. It hangs on to its prey with its jaws as the fast-acting venom kills it.

Inland taipans cope with seasonal changes in temperature by changing colors from season to season. In summer, an inland taipan is pale, which makes its body soak up less heat than dark skin would and helps it keep a little cooler. In winter, it turns dark so it can absorb more heat.

Because its bite is so deadly, the inland taipan is also called the "fierce snake." But it's not actually fierce (unless you're a long-haired rat!). It is shy and would rather be left alone. There is no record of a human death at the fangs of this species.

FACTS

FAMILY Elapidae

OTHER COMMON NAMES Fierce snake, small-scaled snake

SCIENTIFIC NAME *Oxyuranus microlepidotus*

SIZE 5.9 to 8.2 feet (1.8 to 2.5 m)

FOOD Rodents and other small- to medium-size mammals

HABITAT Cracked soil areas in dry, rocky plains

RANGE Western Queensland, northern New South Wales, and northern South Australia in Australia

The fangs of an inland taipan are almost half an inch (1.2 cm) long. These fangs are in the taipan's upper jaw, but sometimes they wear holes in the snake's lower jaw and stick out from below!

NORTHERN COPPERHEAD

FACTS

FAMILY Viperidae

OTHER COMMON NAMES
Copperhead

SCIENTIFIC NAME
Agkistrodon contortrix mokasen

SIZE 22 to 53 inches
(55.9 to 134.6 cm)

FOOD Small mammals, birds,
small reptiles, frogs, insects

HABITAT Woods and rocky
hillsides near lakes, ponds, and
streams; swamps

RANGE Eastern United States
from Massachusetts south to
Georgia and west to Illinois

Young copperheads have bright yellow tail tips. They wiggle their tail tips to lure prey such as frogs, which seem to mistake the tips for worms.

The northern copperhead belongs to a family of snakes called pit vipers. Pit vipers are named for the little pits on their faces that allow them to sense heat. These pit organs can detect the body heat of animals such as mice. Thanks to their pit organs, pit vipers can "see" a heat image of their prey even in pitch darkness.

A hungry copperhead lies still, watching and waiting for prey and then attacking it by surprise. Its bite delivers a deadly dose of venom. The copperhead clamps small prey in its jaws until it's dead and easy to swallow. It lets go of bigger prey to let venom kill it so it can then safely eat its meal without risk of getting injured by its prey's struggles.

Copperheads use a different strategy for insects. They will creep around to find insects and will even climb trees to get them. The snakes are especially likely to show up in places where lots of insects appear at one time. For example, copperheads will arrive in spots where large bugs called cicadas emerge from the ground. The cicadas come out to shed their skins and become adult insects. This all happens in a short span of time, so it's a big feast for the copperheads.

Copperheads spend the winter in big dens packed with dozens of other snakes. Not all of these snakes are copperheads—other species share the den, too. Timber rattlesnakes are often in the mix. Like copperheads, they are venomous pit vipers.

In spring, the snakes emerge. They slither off to find food and mates and to bask on rocks in the sun. Copperheads often lie hidden among leaves, too. Sometimes they shake their tails quickly, which makes the leaves rattle and might function to warn other animals to stay away.

Copperheads of all kinds bite if they feel threatened. These snakes may bite more people each year in the United States than other venomous snakes because they can live near people, holing up in places like woodpiles and old sheds.

Green anacondas are very much at home in the water, where they catch fish and turtles as well as animals that come to get a drink. A female anaconda that is ready to mate is surrounded by many males vying for her attention.

GREEN ANACONDA

The green anaconda is the world's largest snake by weight. It can weigh as much as 550 pounds (227 kg)—about half the weight of a grand piano. It takes a lot of food to fuel a snake like this, and the anaconda is fully capable of killing and swallowing huge meals.

Anacondas are excellent swimmers and hunt in swamps, marshes, and other waterways. A hungry anaconda will lie in ambush underwater with just its eyes and nostrils sticking out of the water. When its unwitting prey comes close, the anaconda seizes it with its jaws. Then it quickly wraps its thick body around its victim.

An anaconda doesn't need venom to kill its prey. Instead, it squeezes with its coiled body, just as all boas do (anacondas are in the boa family). People once thought that boas killed prey by crushing their bones. Then it was suggested that suffocation was the main cause of death. Every time the prey breathed out, the boa's coils tightened until the prey could no longer inhale. In recent years, scientists have shown that the pressure of the boa's coils can actually stop the prey's blood from flowing properly.

Like other boas, the anaconda can tell when its prey has died because its skin can feel when the prey's heart stops. Then the anaconda can eat. Its jaws are linked by elastic cords called ligaments so it can open superwide to fit prey in its mouth— even prey as big as a deer, a pig, or a caiman. Its skin is so stretchy, it can "walk" its mouth over the prey until the entire animal is in its stomach.

A meal that big takes a long time to digest. The anaconda may not eat again for weeks or even months.

FACTS

FAMILY Boidae

OTHER COMMON NAMES Anaconda, common anaconda, water boa

SCIENTIFIC NAME *Eunectes murinus*

SIZE 20 to 30 feet (6 to 9 m)

FOOD Fish, amphibians, reptiles, birds, mammals including deer and capybaras

HABITAT Rain forest rivers, swamps, marshes, flooded grasslands

RANGE Northern South America

Female anacondas are much bigger than male anacondas and can be five times heavier. On rare occasions they have been known to eat male anacondas during the mating season.

RED-TAILED PIPE SNAKE

Giant snakes, and snakes with deadly venom, capture headlines. But the world is filled with smaller snakes that are equally intriguing.

One such snake is the red-tailed pipe snake. Like a lot of snakes, it preys on small animals, such as frogs. It likes soft, damp soil where it can burrow as it searches for grubs and worms to eat. It rotates its small head like a drill as it digs tunnels.

Pipe snakes prey heavily on Brahminy blind snakes, which look like worms. The Brahminy blind snake is also called the flowerpot snake because it has traveled worldwide in plant soil.

Bigger snakes and monitor lizards eat pipe snakes, which have small mouths that aren't much use for biting attackers. Instead, a pipe snake displays behavior that makes it look like a dangerous, venomous cobra.

First, the snake coils its body and flattens it so that it looks wide instead of like a thick pipe. It tucks its head under its body. Then it raises its red-tipped tail in the air. The tail is flattened so that it looks like the spread hood of an angry cobra. By waving around this fake head, a pipe snake may scare away an attacker just long enough to give it a chance to escape. The pipe snake is known in different Asian countries by names that mean "two-headed snake."

Red-tailed pipe snakes are not endangered and survive very well in places where people have moved in and farmed the land. That's probably because these snakes need soft, moist soil for burrowing, and farmland offers this. Pipe snakes also stick near water, so flooded rice paddies are ideal habitats for them. They can even thrive in roadside ditches filled with water.

A red-tailed pipe snake may gleam green, blue, red, and yellow in bright sunlight. The shimmering colors are caused by light reflecting off its scales.

A red-tailed pipe snake has pale bands on its back when it's young. The bands turn red and then darken as the snake ages. An adult's back may be completely black.

This cane toad in its natural South American habitat gulps down a wormlike amphibian called a caecilian. Caecilians are also predators. They eat worms, insects, small reptiles, and frogs.

CANE TOAD

Once upon a time, cane toads were just everyday toads found in Central and South America and a section of Texas. They ate bugs and small animals. In turn, predators ate the cane toads. Cane toads are poisonous, and so are their eggs and tadpoles—poison is their only defense. Poison killed some kinds of the toad's predators, but not all of them. Some animals had adapted so that they weren't harmed by toad poison. Others knew how to avoid the worst parts of the toads' bodies as they fed.

Cane toads aren't a problem in their native lands, but they've become a menace in places where people have released them into the wild. These places have their own naturally occurring wildlife with its balance of predators and prey. Then the cane toad barges in. It gobbles up small animals and munches insects that are the prey of native species. Animals that eat this new toad die. The cane toad is an example of an invasive nonnative species—a species that causes harm in its new habitat.

Why did people release it? Because it was thought that the cane toad would control insects that ate crops. In 1935, for example, about 3,000 cane toads were released in north Queensland in Australia. People hoped they would devour huge numbers of the beetles that ate sugarcane crops.

But the toads didn't have a big impact on beetle populations. However, they made themselves at home and are still spreading across Australia today. Efforts are under way to control this species and encourage citizens to help collect cane toad eggs and capture the toads themselves.

FACTS

FAMILY Bufonidae

OTHER COMMON NAMES
Giant toad, marine toad, giant marine toad, South American cane toad, Dominican toad, spring chicken, shoulder-knot frog

SCIENTIFIC NAME
Rhinella marina

SIZE 4 to 6 inches (10 to 15 cm)

FOOD Insects, snails, small mammals, birds, reptiles, and amphibians

HABITAT Grasslands, open woodlands and forests, gardens, parks, farmlands

RANGE Southern Texas in the United States, tropical Mexico and Central America, northern South America; introduced to Florida and Hawaii in the United States, to Australia, Japan, and many other Pacific and southeast Asian locations

A female cane toad can lay from 8,000 to 17,000 eggs in a single batch. The toads lay eggs in water and can even use just a muddy puddle for this purpose.

People have found horned frogs in the wild that have died because they ate something too big for itself. Sometimes the legs or tails of its prey are even sticking out of a dead frog's mouth.

AMAZONIAN HORNED FROG

If you chose to burrow into a pile of blankets and wait for food to come to you, you'd be feeding a lot like an Amazonian horned frog. This vividly colored frog wiggles itself into the layer of fallen leaves on the floor of its forest home. Then it sits and waits for insects and other prey to come along.

The frog's skin is a jigsaw puzzle of colors that blend in with the leaf litter. Females are dabbed in shades of tan and brown. Males are also tan and brown but are splashed with green as well. Both of them have pointy horns above their eyes. The colors camouflage the frogs from prey as well as from predators that eat frogs, such as birds. The horns may also help with camouflage, as they look a bit like stems or sticks.

When prey gets close, a horned frog pops up from the leaf litter to grab it with its sticky tongue and mouth that can be about one and a half times as wide as its whole body is long. Like a cane toad (pp. 176–177), a horned frog will gobble up whatever it can stuff into its mouth. Most of the time, its meals are ants and beetles, but the frog will also devour prey as big as mice.

The horned frog's mouth is not only big but strong as well. It has tough skin, a beaklike edge, and a few rows of toothlike points. These features help it hold on to its prey once it's caught.

This species and other horned frogs are often called "Pac-Man" frogs because they look and eat a lot like the big-mouthed character in that video game. A horned frog won't hesitate to try to swallow prey that's as big as it is.

FACTS

FAMILY Ceratophryidae

OTHER COMMON NAMES Surinam horned frog, South American horned frog

SCIENTIFIC NAME *Ceratophrys cornuta*

SIZE 2.9 to 8 inches (7.2 to 20 cm)

FOOD Insects, small mammals and reptiles, frogs

HABITAT Freshwater marshes and pools, rain forests

RANGE Northern South America

The tadpoles of horned frogs eat lots of other tadpoles as they grow—even other horned frog tadpoles. Adult horned frogs will eat tadpoles of their own species, as well.

FIRE SALAMANDER

A fire salamander can live for up to 23 years in the wild and 40 years or more in captivity.

A fire salamander's bright colors aren't just for decoration. They are warning signs that tell predators to leave it alone.

Many animals that wear warning signs of black and yellow, orange, or red are either venomous or poisonous. The fire salamander's danger lies in poison glands that sit behind its eyes and dot its body. These glands ooze a thick, sticky fluid from tiny holes, called pores, in its skin. A fire salamander can even spray the fluid for a short distance.

If a predator ignores the warning colors and grabs the salamander, its mouth is filled with pain and a sickening taste. It will most likely drop the salamander as a result.

The poison exists only to protect the salamander. It doesn't use its toxic powers to kill its prey, which consists of invertebrates (boneless animals) such as worms and insects. It finds prey by detecting the motion of a creeping creature. It can also use its sense of smell to find prey, which is important because it feeds at night. It spends most of the day hiding in damp places under stones and logs.

Because fire salamanders like to hide in logs, they sometimes end up in campfires or fireplaces along with the logs. They will quickly dash out when the fire starts. Long ago, people thought the salamanders just popped out of nowhere, which inspired the name "fire salamander."

Salamanders, like all amphibians, need dampness to survive. Many salamanders lay their eggs in water, too, and the larvae live there for a few months before they're ready to move onto land. Some species, however, carry the eggs inside them right up until they're ready to hatch.

Fire salamanders spend the winter hidden away in damp, warm places such as caves. Scientists who study the salamanders have found that they will trek back to the same caves every winter for many years in a row.

TEETH, ZAPS & SLASHING SWORDS

Sailfish work together to herd a school of fish into a small area. Then individual sailfish zip in and out of the school, slashing with their sharp bills. The result? Lots of injured fish for sailfish to grab easily and eat.

ALL ABOUT PREDATORY FISH

Beneath watery waves and ripples lies a world filled with predatory fish. They don't have talons, claws, or beaks for catching prey, but many of them have specialized teeth. Others have snouts and tails that have evolved to become weapons. Some have amazing powers, such as the ability to stun their prey with electrical shocks.

Still other fish use special behaviors to outwit their prey. Some of these behaviors, such as sit-and-wait ambushing, are the same ones used by many land-based predators. Some fish chase their prey.

Various species of fish even lure prey, which is a favorite trick of some reptiles. Some frogfish, for example, wave wormlike lures to attract other fish, just as a snapping turtle does in its freshwater habitat. Many deep-sea fish have built-in fishing rods with glowing tips that attract sea creatures into biting range.

Predatory fish play important roles in keeping their watery habitats healthy. In Shark Bay, Australia, for example, tiger sharks prowl in beds of sea grass. This behavior keeps sea turtles that eat sea grass moving from place to place to avoid the sharks. As a result, the sea turtles don't eat all the sea grass in one place. This is good news for other species that need the sea grass for food and shelter, too.

GOLIATH TIGERFISH
Hydrocynus goliath

The goliath tigerfish lives in lakes and rivers in parts of central Africa. It can measure as much as five feet (1.5 m) long and bites with 32 razor-sharp teeth about the length of your big toe. It's known to hunt in packs to take down large prey. A smaller species of tigerfish even leaps out of the water to snatch birds from the air.

PEACOCK SOLE
Pardachirus pavoninus

The peacock sole is a master of disguise and surprise attacks. Its color and pattern match the seafloor, and it also buries itself in sand. There it lies in wait for small crustaceans, mollusks, and worms. The sole's skin also produces a poisonous fluid that appears to repel sharks when they smell it.

VAMPIRE FISH
Hydrolycus scomberoides

The payara skulks in rivers in parts of South America. Check out its teeth, and you'll see why it's also called the vampire fish. The big fangs sticking out of its lower jaw can be up to six inches (15 cm) long. They slip into spaces in the payara's upper lip when it shuts its mouth. Other fish are speared on these fangs and the rest of the payara's sharp teeth.

SWORDFISH
Xiphias gladius

The swordfish sports a sword on its face. This sword is a superlong upper jawbone. It's also superstrong and capable of piercing a wooden boat hull. Of course, that's not a swordfish's goal! The sword is for hunting. The swordfish doesn't spear prey with its sword. Instead, it slashes at fish to injure and kill them. It gulps prey down whole because it doesn't have any teeth to eat them with.

THRESHER SHARK
Alopias vulpinus

A thresher shark can be up to 24.9 feet (7.6 m) long, with half of that length consisting of its tail. This shark zips toward fish, stops suddenly, and then whips its tail over its head at speeds ranging from 30 to 80 miles an hour (48 to 129 km/h). This attack stuns and smashes apart prey. The shark then easily gobbles up all the bits.

ELECTRIC EEL

FACTS

FAMILY Gymnotidae

OTHER COMMON NAMES None

SCIENTIFIC NAME
Electrophorus electricus

SIZE 6 to 8 feet (1.8 to 2.5 m)

FOOD Fish, small mammals, frogs, crustaceans

HABITAT Muddy waters in marshes, ponds, swamps, and streams

RANGE Northern South America

A male electric eel makes a foamy nest for its mate's eggs. He guards the nest until the young hatch. The first electric eels to hatch may eat siblings that hatch later.

Electric eels really "charge" at their prey! This fish produces electricity in electrical organs that start behind its head and run down the inside of its long body. The organs contain about 6,000 special muscle cells that produce electrical charges. Each cell makes just a little bit, but added up, the cells' power packs a punch.

One organ gives off electricity with a low voltage, which the fish uses to navigate in its dim, muddy habitat. It also uses this electricity to locate fish to eat. The other organs produce much stronger electrical pulses. The fish uses them to kill prey and ward off predators. The jolt from an electric eel is about five times as strong as the power found in a standard North American electrical wall socket.

The electric eel's powerful pulse is thought to be strong enough to knock down a horse. This fish, however, isn't interested in zapping horses. It's after other fish as well as frogs, crabs, and other small water animals. This kind of prey is stunned and paralyzed—or even killed—as the electric eel's zap is conducted by the water.

These zaps can also cause prey that is hiding to twitch and give away its location. The fish uses electricity to keep track of prey as it swims, too. Recently, researchers have shown that an electric eel might also curl its body around larger prey so that its body's electrical fields overlap, making its shocks even stronger.

The electric eel hangs out in shaded areas of the water. This water often has a very low oxygen content, so the eel surfaces to breathe air through its mouth.

Electrical organs fill most of an electric eel's body. The rest of its organs are packed mainly into an area near its head.

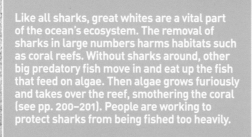

Like all sharks, great whites are a vital part of the ocean's ecosystem. The removal of sharks in large numbers harms habitats such as coral reefs. Without sharks around, other big predatory fish move in and eat up the fish that feed on algae. Then algae grows furiously and takes over the reef, smothering the coral (see pp. 200–201). People are working to protect sharks from being fished too heavily.

GREAT WHITE SHARK

The great white shark is one of the biggest predatory fish in the ocean. It grows to be longer than four baseball bats laid end to end and can weigh as much as a small Asian elephant. It can put on a burst of speed up to 30 miles an hour (48 km/h). Inside its gigantic mouth are rows of razor-sharp teeth—about 300 of them, with around 50 of them ready to tear into prey and the rest lying in wait as they develop. These teeth will take the place of any working teeth that fall out.

Great white sharks eat fish as well as seals and sea lions. Great whites also feast on the floating carcasses of dead whales. Crowds of sharks nuzzle up to the huge meal, with the biggest sharks claiming the best blubbery sections.

A great white finds prey in many ways. It can pick up the scent of blood in the water from a distance of three miles (5 km). Its body also has sensitive skin running down each side that can detect vibrations in the water.

A shark's knifelike teeth enable it to rip big chunks out of large prey. The shark's teeth are not used for chewing—food is gulped down in big pieces.

FACTS

FAMILY Lamnidae

OTHER COMMON NAMES
White shark, white death, maneater

SCIENTIFIC NAME
Carcharodon carcharias

SIZE 13.1 to 23 feet (4 to 7 m)

FOOD Seals, sea lions, elephant seals, dolphins, fish, sea turtles, seabirds, squid, crustaceans, remains of dead whales

HABITAT Tropical to cold ocean waters, often near coasts

RANGE Atlantic, Pacific, and Indian Oceans

A tooth of a great white shark can be more than 2.5 inches (5.7 cm) long.

Greenland sharks' muscles contain chemicals that help them function in extreme cold. These chemicals make their flesh poisonous.

GREENLAND SHARK

The Greenland shark is a strange, little-known shark that lumbers through the cold waters of the northern Atlantic. There it preys on fish, seals, and other sea creatures. It also eats a lot of carrion, including the carcasses of whales. Researchers have found some truly odd animals in the bellies of Greenland sharks, such as horses and an entire reindeer! Most likely, these land animals fell into the sea, drowned, and were later swallowed by the sharks.

This shark definitely lives life in the slow lane due to its cold habitat. It swims slowly as it hunts in deep water, where it's able to catch fairly fast-moving fish as well as seals. It's possible the shark can ambush faster prey in deep water thanks to the low light levels there. It's also possible that these sharks snatch seals when they're sleeping in the water or poking their heads out of the ice to get a breath of air.

This shark grows slowly, too. Scientists estimate that a Greenland shark's length increases as little as .25 to 0.4 inch (.56 to 1 cm) in a year. So how does this shark get so big if it grows so slowly? By living for hundreds of years. Researchers have measured structures in the eyes of dead Greenland sharks that provide clues to an animal's age. One shark appeared to be at least 272 years old. Scientists suggest that the sharks can live as long as 400 years and possibly as much as 500 years.

They're also working to find out how climate change might affect the sharks in their cold subarctic habitat.

FACTS

FAMILY Somniosidae

OTHER COMMON NAMES Sleeper shark, sleeper, gurry shark, ground shark

SCIENTIFIC NAME *Somniosus microcephalus*

SIZE 8 to 24 feet (2.4 to 7.3 m)

FOOD Seals, seabirds, fish, squid, crabs, marine snails, brittle stars, sea urchins, jellyfish, carrion

HABITAT Cold Arctic waters; often found in bays, river mouths, near shore areas; also deeper waters

RANGE Northeastern and northwestern Atlantic Ocean

Many Greenland sharks have a weird, shrimplike crustacean dangling from one or both eyes. This parasite feeds on the sharks' eye and can blind it. However, the sharks live in such dark waters anyway that these pests don't seem to bother them very much.

ATLANTIC TORPEDO

FACTS

FAMILY Torpedinidae

OTHER COMMON NAMES
Great torpedo ray, Atlantic electric ray, black torpedo

SCIENTIFIC NAME
Tetronarce nobiliana

SIZE Up to 5.9 feet (1.8 m)

FOOD Fish, crustaceans, mollusks, worms

HABITAT Sandy or muddy shallow seafloor

RANGE Atlantic Ocean, Mediterranean Sea

Female Atlantic torpedoes are larger than males. (That's typical for species in the elasmobranch group.) A female carries her young inside her body for about a year. She may give birth to as many as 60 young at a time. The little rays often spend their early life living in shallow water and in coral reefs.

The Atlantic torpedo looks rather like a shark that's been flattened by a steamroller. In fact, it's actually related to sharks. The torpedo is a kind of ray, and rays are in the same group of fishes as sharks (the "elasmobranchs"). This group is made up of fish that have skeletons made of a rubbery substance called cartilage, instead of stiff, hard bones.

Most rays swim by flapping their "wings"—the big fins attached to their sides and heads. Not the Atlantic torpedo. It swims by lashing its tail back and forth. Its wings serve a different purpose: They contain the torpedo's secret weapon— a pair of electric organs that it uses to zap its prey.

The Atlantic torpedo waits for prey by sitting on the seafloor. When a fish comes by, the torpedo leaps up and surrounds the fish with its batlike wings. The electric organs, which sit on either side of its head, send out powerful shocks. The shocks hit the fish from all sides and make its nervous system go haywire. Its muscles flinch, and the fish may be stunned or instantly killed. Then the torpedo can easily eat it. A torpedo can kill and eat fish that are quite big considering how small its mouth is, thanks to jaws that open wide.

The torpedo's electrical abilities seem to make it "revolting" to a lot of predators. Few animals dare to go after a big fish that can zap them. A shock from a torpedo is strong enough to stun a human diver into unconsciousness.

Atlantic torpedoes were once caught for use in making oil to light lamps. This oil came from the fish's liver. Today, they're accidentally caught in fishing nets, but they are not purposely caught for food (they're apparently flabby and tasteless!).

A big Atlantic torpedo ray can weigh up to 200 pounds (90 kg). That's about as much as a newborn baby elephant.

Few predators try to tackle fully grown sawfish. Young, small sawfish are eaten by big sharks, dolphins, and crocodiles.

194

LARGETOOTH
SAWFISH

The largetooth sawfish is a kind of ray, like the Atlantic torpedo (pp. 192–193). This puts it in the same group of cartilage-skeleton fish as sharks. It's just not as flat as most kinds of rays. Plus, it's got a giant saw sticking out of its head.

That saw is a good clue to how it hunts. It is actually the sawfish's snout, or rostrum. Lining the saw are sharp, toothlike points. There are 14 to 23 of these points on each side. The sawfish uses its saw to catch fish. It whips the saw from side to side. As the saw strikes, it may stun fish and make them easy to catch, or simply shred them.

The sawfish also uses its saw to poke around in mud and sand underwater. This behavior can turn up shellfish that are hiding. The saw is also dotted with pores that can detect tiny amounts of electricity—the kind that all animals produce just by being alive.

Sawfish have a lifestyle that is different from most rays and sharks. Usually rays and sharks live in salt water, but sawfish are often found in freshwater. They can swim up rivers and into lakes. Today, they're critically endangered worldwide.

Over the past few decades, sawfish populations have gone down by as much as 90 to 99 percent. It's extinct in some of the places where it used to live. One main reason for their decline is the development of coastlines for human use. Mangrove forests are cut down for their wood as well as to make room for farm-land, shrimp farms, hotels, towns, and docks. Unfortunately, sawfish are also hunted for their fins, as are other members of the elasmobranch family. Even the sawfish's useful saw puts it in danger. It easily gets tangled up in fishing nets that are set out to catch other kinds of fish. People are working worldwide to put a stop to this threat to sawfish and other ray species.

FACTS

FAMILY Pristidae

OTHER COMMON NAMES Freshwater sawfish, carpenter shark

SCIENTIFIC NAME *Pristis pristis*

SIZE Up to 23 feet (6.5 m)

FOOD Fish, crustaceans, mollusks

HABITAT Shallow waters of estuaries, river mouths, bays, and along coasts; waters around mangrove forests

RANGE Eastern Atlantic Ocean, western Atlantic Ocean, eastern Pacific Ocean, Indo-West Pacific Ocean

The toothlike points on a sawfish's rostrum are actually specially adapted scales. A sawfish mainly hunts with its saw, but it will also use it to defend itself against predators.

HAIRY FROGFISH

FACTS

FAMILY Antennariidae

OTHER COMMON NAMES
Striated frogfish, striped frogfish, zebra frogfish, splitlure frogfish, striate anglerfish

SCIENTIFIC NAME
Antennarius striatus

SIZE 4 to 9.8 inches (10 to 25 cm)

FOOD Fish, crustaceans

HABITAT Rocky reefs, coral reefs, sea grass meadows, tide pools in coastal waters

RANGE Atlantic Ocean, Indian Ocean, western Pacific Ocean

The hairy frogfish has a stretchy stomach and can swallow fish that are twice its size. Its large mouth is also an important feature that allows it to eat lionfish, which have long, venomous spines.

A hairy frogfish looks like a bowl of spaghetti crossed with a sock puppet. It looks as if it's always prepared to go to a costume party. But it's really just always ready to slurp up prey.

This fish's weird appearance is actually excellent camouflage. Its frilly covering makes it look like a clump of seaweed. It can also slowly change color over several weeks to match its habitat. As a result, these fish can be a range of colors—tan, orange, yellow, and even black—and sport many stripes, spots, and blotches, or none at all.

Cloaked in this disguise, the frogfish can sit and wait to launch a surprise attack on fish and other prey that don't notice it. But it also has another trick. On top of its head is a built-in fishing lure. Dangling from the lure are two to seven fleshy bits that look like worms. A hungry frogfish wiggles these worms to attract prey right up to its face.

Then the prey is in for a nasty surprise. A frogfish has a huge mouth, and it quickly opens wide. The prey is sucked in as if the frogfish were a vacuum cleaner. Then the fish slams its jaws shut. All of this happens in just six milliseconds—too fast for the eye to see! Nobody knew exactly how this fish caught its prey before high-speed cameras were invented.

A female frogfish is bigger than a male. She has to be, because her body may contain as many as 180,000 eggs when it comes time to lay them. The freshly laid eggs stick together in a long, jellylike clump that can float in the water. This clump is called an egg raft. The egg raft is able to float long distances in the sea, which helps this species spread out in its habitat.

Frogfish have fins that they use as legs to scramble across the seafloor. They can even hop and walk with them.

The skinny "fishing rod" on a viperfish's back is the front ray of its dorsal (back) fin. It is tipped with a glowing lure that attracts prey right to the viperfish's mouth. A viperfish can go without food for about 12 days after it eats a big meal.

SLOANE'S VIPERFISH

You might not want to ask a Sloane's viperfish to smile for the camera. This is a fish with one gruesome grin. It has the largest teeth compared to its head size of any animal. The needle-sharp teeth in its jaws are more than half as long as its head. They stick out like quills when the fish shuts its mouth.

This eerie fish lives in the dark depths of the ocean, where it ripples through the water like a snake. Along its sides gleam rows of light-producing cells. These cells make light by way of a chemical reaction in much the same way as a firefly's body does.

Many fish migrate upward in the ocean at night to feed, and the viperfish takes advantage of this behavior. It migrates upward, too, and lurks to grab other fish. It can even pierce its prey with its teeth just by swimming quickly toward it.

A viperfish also dangles a lure over its head to attract fish. Any fish that comes near will be gulped down by the viperfish, which can open its mouth incredibly wide. Its fangs are hinged in a way that lets it use them like prison bars to keep struggling prey in its mouth.

Food can be hard to find in the deep, dark waters of the ocean, so fish that live here must make the most of the meals they find. The viperfish, like many other species, has a stomach that can stretch to hold a supersize meal. It can swallow prey more than half as long as its body.

Little is known about fish that live at great depths, but it's thought that the viperfish also uses its lights to communicate with other viperfish, especially when it seeks a mate.

FACTS

FAMILY Stomiidae

OTHER COMMON NAMES Needletooth, Dannevig's dragonfish, Sloane's fangfish, many-light viperfish

SCIENTIFIC NAME *Chauliodus sloani*

SIZE Up to 14 inches (35 cm)

FOOD Fish, crustaceans

HABITAT Tropical and temperate oceans

RANGE Worldwide

Most fish have skulls and spines that are strongly connected, but the viperfish has a special joint in its head that allows it to open its mouth extremely wide. The joint lets it flip its skull back and jut its lower jaw forward to seize and swallow prey.

ATLANTIC GOLIATH GROUPER

FACTS

FAMILY Epinephelidae

OTHER COMMON NAMES
Giant seabass, black bass

SCIENTIFIC NAME
Epinephelus itajara

SIZE Up to 8.2 feet (2.5 m)

FOOD Fish, crabs

HABITAT Coral reefs, mangrove forests

RANGE Tropical and temperate waters in the Atlantic Ocean and eastern Pacific Ocean

When it comes to noisy animals, you don't usually think of fish. But the Atlantic goliath grouper makes its displeasure known with a loud rumbling sound. It makes this noise by pumping its swim bladder, an air-filled organ inside it that helps it float. The rumble usually means "go away"!

The goliath grouper is one big fish. It is about half as long as a typical station wagon and can weigh as much as 1,000 pounds (455 kg). Because it's so big, it can eat big prey, including the smaller species of sharks. The grouper just opens its big mouth wide, which causes water and prey to flow inside.

But like all fish, the grouper starts out small. The tiny hatchlings become little fish about an inch (2.5 cm) long. These mini-groupers spend their first few years growing up in sheltered places, such as shallow bays. A favorite grouper "nursery" is a mangrove forest, where the trees' roots provide good hiding places for the young fish. They move to coral reefs when they get older and bigger.

Groupers are good caretakers of coral reefs, even if they don't know it. The big fish eat a lot of other predatory fish. This helps algae-eating fish thrive. These fish, in turn, keep algae from covering the reef and suffocating the corals. As a result, the reef is a healthy, productive place that is able to support lots of animals.

For a goliath grouper, its reef is home sweet home. It doesn't travel to other places or go exploring—except during breeding season. Then a grouper may swim as far as 300 miles (483 km) to join up with a group of groupers.

In most species of groupers, female fish can turn into male fish over the course of their lives. They cannot, however, go back to being female.

GREEN MORAY
EEL

Imagine a sea monster that has not one, but two sets of jaws. One set grabs fish as they swim. The other set is hidden in the throat. This second set shoots forward, sinks its teeth into the trapped fish, and finishes the job of dragging it into the monster's gullet.

It sounds like a horror movie—but fish called moray eels really do have two sets of jaws. These eels aren't monsters. They're just hungry sea creatures. These long, snakelike fish live in the nooks and crannies of a coral reef, where space is tight. They don't have much wiggle room to open their mouths really wide to suck in large prey the way many fish in open waters can.

Instead, a moray eel grabs prey with its teeth. Then the eel uses its second set of jaws, which are called pharyngeal jaws. ("Pharyngeal" refers to the pharynx, the part of the throat right behind the mouth.) The eel can stick these jaws into its mouth to haul prey down its throat.

The green moray eel is one of the largest of these double-jawed wonders. Its green color is due to a thick layer of gooey yellow mucus that covers its grayish brown body. The mucus helps protect it from pests that live on fish skin. Like other reef dwellers, the green moray also visits "cleaning stations" on the reef where cleaner shrimps and tiny fish called wrasses nibble pests off bigger fish.

A green moray prowls at night, poking into crevices and between rocks to look for prey. It uses its sense of smell to locate food. By day, it sits inside its rocky home with just its head sticking out. It can also hunt this way, staying put until it can launch a surprise attack on a passing fish.

FACTS

FAMILY Muraenidae

OTHER COMMON NAMES
Green conger, black moray, olive-green moray

SCIENTIFIC NAME
Gymnothorax funebris

SIZE 6 to 8 feet (1.8 to 2.5 m)

FOOD Fish, crustaceans, squid

HABITAT Tidepools, rocky shores, mangroves, coral reefs, sea grass beds

RANGE Western Atlantic Ocean including the Gulf of Mexico and the Caribbean Sea

This x-ray shows a moray eel's two sets of jaws. Most fish with pharyngeal jaws use them to crush prey in their throats. Unlike a moray, they can't propel the jaws into their mouths to bite.

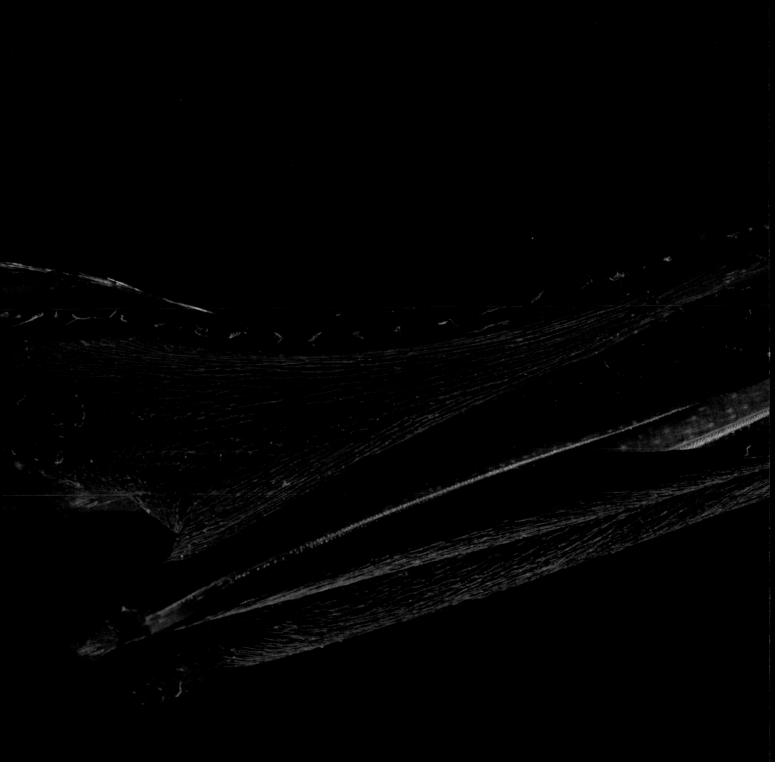

A pelican eel may have an extremely big mouth, but its teeth are tiny. It mainly feeds on small crustaceans.

PELICAN EEL

No other animal is quite like a pelican eel. In fact, it truly is one of a kind: It is the only species in its group, or family, of living things.

A pelican eel is pretty much just a swimming mouth. Its jaws make up 25 percent of its total length. The jaws are linked by skin that folds up like an umbrella's cloth when the jaws are shut, and spreads wide when they are open.

It's thought that the fish spreads its giant mouth wide as it lunges toward its prey. All the water pushing against the skin of its mouth stretches it extra wide. Suddenly the eel's mouth is many times larger than the rest of its body put together.

The giant mouth then simply surrounds the prey, the way you might grab jelly beans from a bowl and then make a fist. The jelly beans, however, aren't as messy as an eel meal, because the eel has to squeeze out all the water before it swallows.

Having a big mouth and a stretchy stomach lets the eel gorge on a source of food when it finds it, which isn't always easy in deep water. Other than that gaping mouth, the eel consists of a pair of little eyes perched near its nose. Its skull is very small, as if it's just something from which to hang its jaws. Behind its small body trails a very long tail, which is tipped with a pinkish white organ that glows to lure prey.

As if all this isn't enough, the pelican eel also lacks the scales that cover most fishes' bodies. Instead, its body is covered with black, velvety skin.

FACTS

FAMILY Eurypharyngidae

OTHER COMMON NAMES
Gulper eel, pelican fish, big-mouth gulper, deep-sea gulper eel, umbrella mouth gulper

SCIENTIFIC NAME
Eurypharynx pelecanoides

SIZE Up to 40 inches (100 cm)

FOOD Fish, squid, crustaceans

HABITAT Deep sea

RANGE Worldwide in tropical and temperate oceans

A male pelican eel grows an extra big nose when he is ready to find a mate. This is a clue that perhaps a male finds a female by using his sense of smell. His teeth and jaws also seem to wither away, possibly indicating that males die after mating.

The hump on a humphead wrasse's face gets larger as the fish ages. The biggest humps are sported by large, dominant males called supermales.

HUMPHEAD WRASSE

Crunch! Chomp! Crack! **That's what scuba divers** sometimes hear when they explore coral reefs inhabited by the humphead wrasse. This big fish has teeth that are fused to form a beak that is rather like a parrot's. The wrasse uses its strong beak to feed on crabs, sea stars, and other animals with hard shells or tough outer skeletons, called exoskeletons.

As if a sharp beak wasn't enough, the wrasse also has teeth in its throat. Many species of fish do—even goldfish. Teeth like this are called pharyngeal teeth. A wrasse can't move its pharyngeal teeth into its mouth the way a moray eel can (pp. 202–203). But it can use them to continue the job of crunching shellfish that was started by its beak. The teeth are also handy for crushing coral to eat the small worms and other animals hiding in them.

Humphead wrasses seem to have an appetite for hard-to-stomach foods—they are among the few species that can eat poisonous prey such as boxfish and sluglike animals called sea hares. They even dine on crown-of-thorns sea stars, which are covered with venomous spines.

A humphead wrasse can live for up to 32 years, but today few wrasse make it to that age. Many countries that are home to humphead wrasses have passed laws to protect them, but illegal hunting (called poaching) still goes on. The poachers catch young, small wrasses. The rare fish will be sold for high prices in fish markets.

Governments, researchers, and other people are working to stop this trade.

FACTS

FAMILY Labridae

OTHER COMMON NAMES Humphead, giant wrasse, Maori wrasse, truck wrasse

SCIENTIFIC NAME *Cheilinus undulatus*

SIZE 2 to 7.5 feet (0.6 to 2.3 m)

FOOD Fish, crustaceans, mollusks, sea urchins, sea stars

HABITAT Coral reefs, sea grass beds, mangrove areas, lagoons

RANGE Tropical Indian Ocean and Pacific Ocean

Female humphead wrasses are red-orange. Males are vivid green-blue. Some females turn into males when they are between 9 and 15 years old and change their color, too.

REEF LIZARDFISH

FACTS

FAMILY Synodontidae

OTHER COMMON NAMES
Variegated lizardfish, red lizardfish, two-spot lizardfish, scaly-cheek lizardfish, short-nosed lizardfish, Engleman's lizardfish

SCIENTIFIC NAME
Synodus variegatus

SIZE 6 to 9 inches (14 to 24 cm)

FOOD Fish, shrimps

HABITAT Coral reefs, lagoons

RANGE Indian Ocean, Pacific Ocean, Red Sea, coastal Hawaii

Sit. Wait. *Snap!* Sit. Wait. *Snap!* The reef lizardfish is one of the many predators that uses the old sit-and-wait ambush way of grabbing prey. It boasts many adaptations for this kind of life.

For a start, it's not easy for prey to see the lizardfish. Its speckled pattern makes it blend in with its surroundings. The lizardfish will also partly bury itself if necessary to make sure it's hard to see. This camouflage also conceals the lizardfish from its own predators.

The lizardfish can sit perfectly still for long periods of time. It props itself up with its sturdy, leglike fins and bends its back so that it's gazing upward. This posture gives it its name of lizardfish, because it looks a lot like a lizard basking on a rock.

That explains the sitting and waiting parts of its predatory behavior. The *snap!* comes when a school of small fish swims by. The alert lizardfish bursts out of hiding to reveal a very big mouth filled with extremely sharp, pointy teeth. These teeth cover its lips and even its tongue. In the blink of an eye, a fish becomes dinner in its jaws.

There are more than 50 different species of lizardfish. One especially sneaky species, known as the sand-diver lizardfish, will lie in wait near places on a reef where little cleaner shrimps have "cleaning stations" (pp. 202–203). Fish stop at these stations to let the shrimps clean pests off their skin. That's when the lizardfish leaps out of hiding to attack the unsuspecting fish.

The gracile lizardfish blends in perfectly with pebbles and sand. This camouflage hides it from the eyes of predators as well as humans. However, researchers have recently found that it glows lime green when they shine blue light on it.

What a mouthful! A lizardfish typically swallows other fish headfirst, as most animals do when they eat fish. A fish is just easier to swallow that way because its streamlined body slips down smoothly. This lizardfish, however, isn't giving up even if it mistakenly gobbled its prey tail-first!

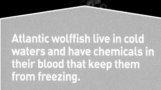

Atlantic wolffish live in cold waters and have chemicals in their blood that keep them from freezing.

ATLANTIC WOLFFISH

Grr! **An Atlantic wolffish may look as if it's** growling like a hungry wolf, but it's only deadly if you are a creature with a shell or an exoskeleton. That's because a wolffish's teeth are adapted for crushing and eating animals such as lobsters, crabs, sea stars, sea urchins, and snails.

The wolffish has thick, cone-shaped, doglike teeth in the front of both its upper and lower jaws. Behind them are rows of sturdy, domed teeth a bit like your molar teeth. Teeth jut from its throat as well. These no-nonsense teeth are set in a heavy head equipped with mighty jaws. All these features help a wolffish to feast on its armored prey.

A wolffish prowls reefs and rocky seafloors to find its slow-moving prey. It grabs prey with sharp teeth that stick out of its mouth and then crushes its shell with the domed teeth. Then it swallows its meal, broken bits of shell and all! Crunching up seashells is hard on teeth, however, so the Atlantic wolffish sheds its worn-out teeth and grows a new set every year.

Wolffish grow up slowly and don't find mates until they're about six years old. Then a male and female wolffish pair up for the breeding season. The female can lay between 5,000 and 12,000 eggs. The male guards the eggs for months until they hatch. He doesn't eat during this time.

Scientists and people in the fishing industry are working to learn more about wolffish and how to protect them.

FACTS

FAMILY Anarhichadidae

OTHER COMMON NAMES Sea wolf, Atlantic catfish, ocean catfish, devil fish, wolf eel, sea cat

SCIENTIFIC NAME *Anarhichas lupus*

SIZE Up to 5 feet (1.5 m)

FOOD Mollusks, crustaceans, echinoderms

HABITAT Sea grass beds, rocky areas

RANGE Northern Atlantic Ocean

Atlantic wolffish have bitten people who have caught them, but they are not typically dangerous to people. They will usually swim away from divers and hide in their dens. The long, ribbonlike body of a swimming wolffish makes it look like an eel.

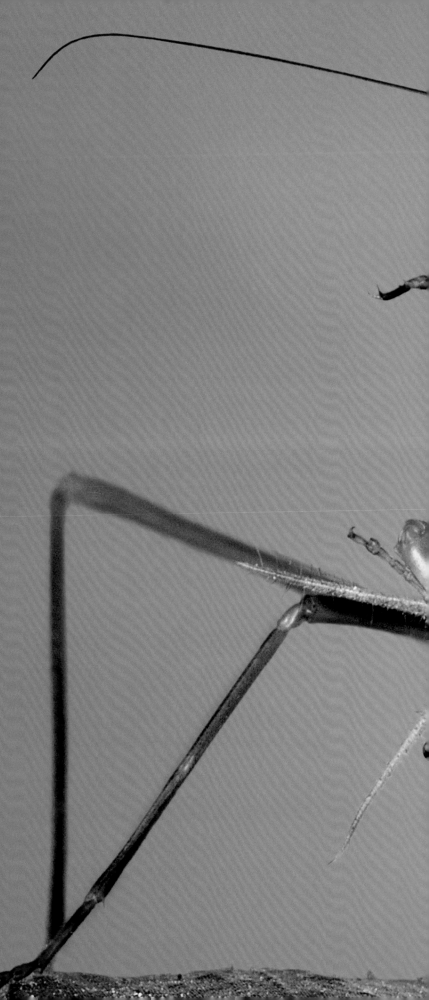

STINGS, BITES & TRICKY TRAPS

This nymph of a Chinese mantis, a species of praying mantis native to China, is eating a cricket while standing on a leaf.

213

ALL ABOUT PREDATORY INVERTEBRATES

Scorpions, spiders, and squid, oh my! The world of invertebrates—animals without backbones—is enormous. About 97 percent of all animals are invertebrates. Animals in this group boast some of the weirdest, wildest shapes, body parts, and behaviors in the animal kingdom. If you want to make up creatures for a science-fiction story, just look at invertebrates for inspiration!

Invertebrates are divided into eight groups. The biggest group is made up of insects—there are more than one million known species. The other seven groups include a wide variety of animals, such as snails, worms, spiders, sea stars, and sponges.

Many invertebrates are plant-eaters or filter feeders (animals that filter tiny particles, including bacteria, from water). There are also many predatory invertebrates. Some of them are active hunters that seek out prey. Others set traps to catch their prey and then attack their victims. Still others use that old favorite, ambush predation—hiding, sitting, and waiting for prey to wander by, sometimes throwing in a lure to speed things up.

Here are just a few incredible invertebrate predators.

GIANT PACIFIC OCTOPUS
Enteroctopus dofleini

With the size of its arms, the giant Pacific octopus can span as much as 30 feet (9.1 m). It feeds by suddenly draping prey such as fish, clams, or lobsters with its sucker-lined arms and dragging it into its mouth, where it's torn to bits by a razor-sharp beak. This octopus has even been known to catch sharks!

ASSASSIN BUG
Platymeris biguttata

Most assassin bugs prey on other invertebrates. An assassin bug kills prey by jabbing it with its long snout and injecting it with deadly fluids. The fluid turns the prey's insides to a soup that the bug can suck out.

LION'S MANE JELLYFISH
Cyanea capillata

The lion's mane jellyfish has hundreds of long tentacles dangling from its blobby body. Each tentacle is packed with stinging cells that are like tiny harpoons. Fish and other prey are stunned by the venom in these harpoons when they're stung. Then the jellyfish drags the prey into its bell-shaped body to digest it.

GIANT WHIP SCORPION
Mastigoproctus giganteus

The giant whip scorpion's name makes it sound very scary. But this predator is only a deadly giant if you're an insect or worm. This creature is about two inches (5 cm) long. That doesn't include its "whip," which works like an antenna and helps it hunt crickets, termites, and other invertebrates at night.

EUROPEAN GARDEN SPIDER
Araneus diadematus

You can easily find a garden spider in a typical park or garden in Europe and North America—or at least its web. This spider and its web are an everyday example of an amazing kind of predation. The garden spider is one of many spider species that make silk and spin it into a sticky web that captures insects.

A female crown-of-thorns sea star can contain up to 24 million eggs in her body at one time. In just one breeding season, she can produce 60 to 100 million eggs.

CROWN-OF-THORNS SEA STAR

A sea star is a kind of echinoderm—an animal with an outer skeleton covered by tough skin that ranges from soft to very hard. Sea urchins, sand dollars, and sea cucumbers are echinoderms, too.

The word "echinoderm" means "spiny skin." Not all echinoderms have spiny skin, but the crown-of-thorns sea star is like a living pincushion. This big sea star has between seven and 23 arms that flare out from its body. It's covered with sturdy spines that can be up to two inches (5 cm) long. The skin on the spines contains venom that protects it from predators.

The crown-of-thorns sea star hunts by creeping over a coral reef. When it senses that it's lying on top of its meal, it settles in to eat: Its stomach pushes out of its body and drapes itself over its prey. Digestive juices ooze out to break down the food, which is then absorbed by the sea star's stomach.

This species feeds heavily on coral species that can replace themselves quickly, so normally it does not harm its habitat.

If there are very large numbers of these sea stars, however, they eat all the fast-growing coral. Then they start feeding on the slower-growing kinds. The coral animals (called polyps) can't reproduce fast enough to keep up with the hungry sea stars. As a result, large areas of the reef are stripped of living coral. This, in turn, affects other animals that depend on healthy coral reefs to survive.

FACTS

FAMILY Acanthasteridae

OTHER COMMON NAMES Crown-of-thorns starfish, COTS

SCIENTIFIC NAME *Acanthaster planci*

SIZE 9.8 to 31.8 inches (25 to 80 cm)

FOOD Stony corals, soft corals, sponges, carrion, algae

HABITAT Coral reefs

RANGE Indian Ocean, Pacific Ocean

A single crown-of-thorns sea star can eat a patch of coral the size of its own body in just one night. That adds up to 140 square feet (13 sq m) in a year—an area about the size of a typical living room in a house.

GIANT TRITON

FACTS

FAMILY Ranellidae

OTHER COMMON NAMES
Triton's trumpet

SCIENTIFIC NAME
Charonia tritonis

SIZE Up to 20 inches (50 cm)

FOOD Sea slugs, sea snails, sea stars, sea cucumbers

HABITAT Coral reefs, sand flats

RANGE Tropical Indian Ocean and Pacific Ocean from East Africa to Hawaii

It's hard to imagine a snail chasing its prey.

The fastest land snail, after all, takes an hour to travel just 3.3 feet (1 m). But a slow-motion high-speed chase is fine for the giant triton. That's because this big sea snail chases equally slow-moving prey, mainly sea slugs, sea stars, and other sea snails.

The giant triton detects its prey using its sense of smell. It goes after it, creeping along on its giant, muscular foot. That foot is also used to grab its prey. Then the triton starts scraping its prey with a rough, tongue-like mouthpart called the radula. The radula is covered with thousands of toothy spikes.

As the triton files away at its victim, its venomous saliva flows into its prey and paralyzes it so it can't escape or fight back. Then the triton can easily use its radula to strip flesh off its prey and eat it.

The giant triton is one of the only sea creatures that feeds on the crown-of-thorns sea star (pp. 216–217). The sea star is aware of this—when it smells a triton, it immediately scrambles to "run" away. Some researchers are looking into using chemicals that copy the scent of a giant triton to control these coral-eating sea stars on fragile coral reefs.

The beautiful shell of the giant triton has fascinated people for hundreds of years. Since the 1930s, however, populations of giant tritons have dropped steeply because people collected them for their shells. Today, the triton is very rare. It is a protected species in many places.

Various triton-snail species lay eggs contained in packages called capsules. This hairy triton *(Fusitriton cancellatus)* is on her egg mass in South America's Patagonia. A female giant triton's egg capsule may contain hundreds of eggs.

Old, empty triton shells have been used as trumpets since ancient times in many Pacific Ocean lands, such as Japan, New Zealand, and Fiji.

The part of a colossal squid's body that contains its stomach is full of a thick, dark red coloring. The squid eats deep-sea fish that produce light, but the red substance stops the glowing meals from shining through the squid's body and making it visible to predators.

COLOSSAL SQUID

The giant squid is a huge animal longer than a school bus. Yet deep in the ocean lurks the colossal squid, which may be even longer and heavier. Nobody knows for sure because this mysterious creature has only rarely been spotted or caught.

In 2007, fishers near Antarctica accidentally caught a colossal squid while fishing. The fishers were the first to ever see a living colossal squid. They dragged it on board and brought it to New Zealand for study. The squid weighed in at 1,091 pounds (495 kg)—about as much as four pro-football players. It measured about 33 feet (10 m) long.

Though nobody knows just how colossal the colossal squid can be, scientists do know that it has the biggest eyes of any animal. A single eye measures 10.6 inches (27 cm) across. Each one is about as big as a soccer ball. Under the eyes are double rows of light-producing organs. The lights may fool prey into thinking the squid is just another glowing fish. Oddly, the lights may also help hide the squid as it swims up from the deep sea. The light shining from below its eyes matches the light streaming down from above and makes the eyes coming closer harder for prey to see.

The colossal squid also has sharp hooks that swivel on the tips of its two long feeding tentacles. These vicious tools drag fish and other prey to the squid's mouth, which contains an enormous, razor-sharp beak.

The colossal squid has left round scars with their suckers on the skin of sperm whales (pp. 110–111), which feast on these big invertebrates. Scientists have also found the beaks of colossal squid in sperm whales' stomachs.

FACTS

FAMILY Cranchiidae

OTHER COMMON NAMES Giant cranch squid

SCIENTIFIC NAME *Mesonychoteuthis hamiltoni*

SIZE Unknown; possibly up to 46 feet (14 m) or more, including tentacles

FOOD Fish, squid

HABITAT Deep, cold oceans

RANGE Atlantic Ocean, Indian Ocean, Pacific Ocean around Antarctica

Scientists think that just one Patagonian toothfish weighing about as much as a medium-size bowling ball is enough food to keep a colossal squid alive for nearly 200 days.

This army ant is a soldier—you can tell by its supersize mandibles. A soldier's job is to bite any animal that threatens the colony.

ARMY ANT

If you were a bug, you wouldn't want to be crossing the road when a platoon of army ants approaches. When these insects go on patrol, they eat just about everything in their path.

There are more than 200 species of ants that are known as army ants, but the best known and most studied species is *Eciton burchellii* of Central and South America.

Army ants' long legs are tipped with hooks. Thousands of ants build a temporary "nest" by linking up with each other using the hooks on their legs. They don't build underground nests because they move to a new place every few weeks to find new food sources. As a result, their nests need to be more like tents than houses.

In the middle of this clump of ants is the queen, who lays all the eggs and is the mother of all the ants. Young, undeveloped ants called larvae are kept in the middle, too.

Food is obtained by worker ants, which go on raids at night. As many as 200,000 ants fan out across a wide area. They work in groups to sting prey and tear it apart with their hooked jaws, or mandibles.

Insects and other prey respond to this invasion in different ways. Some animals freeze in place, because the ants are nearly blind and might not detect them if they don't move. Some hide, while others fight back with ant-repelling chemicals.

A colony of army ants can contain as many as two million ants. These ants have different jobs, and look different depending on the jobs they do. Very small ants take care of the eggs and young. Soldier ants, which are like guards, have extra big heads and mandibles. Worker ants, smaller than soldiers, make up the largest group.

FACTS

FAMILY Formicidae

OTHER COMMON NAMES Burchell's army ant, legionary ant

SCIENTIFIC NAME *Eciton burchellii*

SIZE .12 to .47 inch (3 to 12 mm)

FOOD Insects, arachnids, small reptiles, amphibians

HABITAT Forests

RANGE Tropical Central and South America

Two army ants work to carry food back to the nest. Ant larvae need high-fat meals, and the workers often feed them the larvae of different insect species—including those of other kinds of ants.

TWELVE-SPOTTED SKIMMER

FACTS

FAMILY Libellulidae

OTHER COMMON NAMES
Ten-spotted skimmer

SCIENTIFIC NAME
Libellula pulchella

SIZE 1.8 to 2.3 inches
(4.5 to 5.8 cm)

FOOD Insects (as adult)

HABITAT Ponds, lakes,
marshes, streams

RANGE Southern Canada,
lower 48 United States

A dragonfly has about 30,000 lenses in each of its huge, round compound eyes. It can see around it in nearly all directions. Its eyes are very sensitive to motion, which both helps it catch prey and avoid being caught.

The twelve-spotted skimmer is a kind of dragonfly. It belongs to a large group of insects that includes more than 5,000 known species of dragonflies and damselflies. Each of its four wings has three dark spots. These twelve spots give it its name.

Like other dragonflies, the twelve-spot starts life as an egg laid in water. The egg hatches into a fierce little predator called a naiad. A naiad lives underwater, where it sits and waits to snare prey such as insect larvae, tiny shrimps, tadpoles, and even little fish. It's equipped for this task with a lower jaw that shoots out and snags prey with a set of bristles on its tip.

When a naiad is fully grown, it emerges from the water and starts its life as a flying insect. Dragonflies are the flying aces of the insect world. They can zip along at speeds up to 30 miles an hour (48 km/h). They can move each wing independently, turn on a dime, hover in one place, and even fly backward and upside down.

Dragonflies are also more successful hunters than some of the world's most famous predators. Studies show that lions only catch about 25 percent of the prey they go after, and nearly half of a great white shark's attempts are failures. Polar bears succeed about 10 percent of the time, and peregrine falcons catch their prey about half of the time. But dragonflies have a success rate of more than 95 percent!

A dragonfly hunts by watching for motion with its huge eyes. It zooms up from just behind and below its prey and snares it with its feet. Then its sharp jaws get to work crunching and mashing up its meal, which it often eats while flying.

PRAYING MANTIS

FACTS

FAMILY Mantidae

OTHER COMMON NAMES
European mantid

SCIENTIFIC NAME
Mantis religiosa

SIZE 2 to 3 inches (5 to 7.6 cm)

FOOD Insects

HABITAT Meadows, fields, gardens, parks, pastures

RANGE Europe, North America, Asia, Africa

A mantis has a very flexible neck. Unlike other insects, it can swivel its head around much like a person does.

The praying mantis gets its name from the way it holds its front legs in a bent position, as if it were praying. But you can definitely call it a *preying* mantis, because that's really why the mantis holds its legs that way. It's ready to seize the next unsuspecting insect that bumbles by.

The mantis hunts by sitting perfectly still or slowly sneaking up on prey. Its color, which ranges from tan to green, blends in perfectly with twigs and leaves. When prey is finally within reach, the mantis's front legs snap forward and seize the prey. Spikes on its legs trap the prey, which the mantis starts eating.

The praying mantis is a European species of mantid, but it found its way to North America in 1899 when it arrived as a stowaway in nursery plants. When a nonnative animal turns up in this way in a new country, it can often cause problems in its new habitat, but the praying mantis never became a problem. Instead, it proved to be a helpful insect that eats pests in gardens.

There are about 2,000 species of mantids. They come in a wide variety of colors and shapes. Many of them are green or brown, like the praying mantis. Some species of mantids that live in tropical areas sport bright colors such as pink and orange. These colors help them blend in with tropical flowers. They sit and wait for nectar-sipping insects to come close to the flowers.

Other mantids are shaped and colored so that they look like dead leaves, clumps of thorns, and even wasps. Some mantids are so big that they can catch little frogs and lizards as well as hummingbirds.

Mantids often eat others of their own species. Baby mantids, called nymphs, eagerly chow down on other nymphs. A female mantis sometimes devours her mate. In this picture, the praying mantis is eating a grasshopper.

When a green tiger beetle catches its prey, it squashes and snips its victim with its giant, sharp, jagged mandibles. As it slices and dices, it oozes digestive fluids onto its meal.

GREEN TIGER BEETLE

The green tiger beetle looks like a jewel, with its metallic green color that gleams in the sunlight. It's one spectacular insect!

But it's also amazing when it is just a dull-colored, tubby larva—at least when it comes to searching for prey. This larva digs a burrow in loose, sandy soil. Then it lies inside the burrow in the opening. Hooks on its back are jabbed into the sides of the burrow, keeping the larva firmly stuck in place so it can't be pulled out. Any prey passing by is quickly seized by the larva's large mandibles and dragged into the burrow.

However, the larva can be overcome by another predator—a little ant-size wasp that is able to avoid its jaws and slip into its burrow. The wasp yanks the larva deeper into the burrow and stings it. The sting paralyzes the larva, and the wasp lays eggs on it. Later, newly hatched wasps eat the larva.

That would never happen to an adult green tiger beetle, though! The adult shifts from being an ambush predator to running after its prey. The beetle has long legs for running fast. As a result, tiger beetles are the sprint champions among insects. The green tiger beetle's "cousin," the Australian tiger beetle, is the fastest running insect in the world. It can hit speeds of more than five miles an hour (8 km/h). That's faster than most people walk.

Tiger beetles run so fast that their eyesight can't keep up. The beetle's big eyes can't collect the light they need to form a clear picture of its prey. So it has to stop and focus again before continuing its chase. It holds its antennae out in front of it to sense objects it might otherwise trip over.

FACTS

FAMILY Carabidae

OTHER COMMON NAMES None

SCIENTIFIC NAME *Cicindela campestris*

SIZE 0.5 to 0.6 inch (1.2 to 1.5 cm)

FOOD Insects, spiders

HABITAT Heathlands, dunes, hillsides, open grounds

RANGE Europe

The largest tiger beetle species is the African giant tiger beetle. It can be as much as 2.1 inches (5.4 cm) in length, with powerful hooked mandibles in front that make it look like a forklift.

DEVIL'S COACH HORSE

FACTS

FAMILY Staphylinidae

OTHER COMMON NAMES
Cock-tail beetle, rove beetle

SCIENTIFIC NAME *Ocypus olens*

SIZE 0.8 to 1.3 inches
(2 to 3.2 cm)

FOOD Insects, spiders, slugs,
snails, worms, wood lice, carrion

HABITAT Woodlands, parks,
gardens

RANGE Europe, North Africa,
North America, Australasia

With a name like devil's coach horse, you might expect this beetle to be a danger to humans. But it's actually a very good insect to have in a garden because it eats a lot of insect pests as well as slugs and snails that munch on plants.

A snail's shell is excellent armor, so how does a little beetle manage to kill it? Scientists found that the devil's coach horse could snap off bits of the shell to attack the soft snail body inside. If you find empty snail shells with holes in the side, you may have found a clue that a devil's coach horse was there.

The devil's coach horse most likely got its strange name because it looks menacing. It has big, curved mandibles, which it uses to catch and cut up its prey. (If it bites a person that picks it up, the nip feels like a pinch.) It also lifts the tip of its abdomen over its back like a skunk if it feels threatened. It has two glands in its abdomen that can emit a very stinky fluid, so a predator that wants to eat the beetle might think twice before attacking it.

The devil's coach horse's natural habitat is in Europe and North Africa. It has also spread to other parts of the world, such as North America. It's believed that it was first accidentally released into California in the 1920s.

In a laboratory setting, a devil's coach horse ate 20 garden snails in 22 days. That means it ate nearly its own weight in snails every day. That's like an average 11-year-old kid eating 320 quarter-pound burgers in a day.

This devil's coach horse beetle is arched in a defensive pose. The droplet on the tip of its abdomen is a smelly fluid that helps repel predators.

GIANT WATER BUG

Ouch! **That's the sound of a swimmer wading in** a pond who has nearly stepped on a giant water bug—and revealing why it's also called a "toe-biter."

Giant water bugs don't actually prey on toes. What they are after are small water creatures. The bug hunts by waiting for prey to move into striking range. Then the bug springs at its prey and grabs it with its curved front legs.

Next, it stabs its long beak into the prey's body. Digestive juices flow into the prey to break it down and turn it into a soupy mess that the bug can slurp up and swallow. The bug waits for a few minutes for this "meltdown" to take place before it starts feeding. When it's done, it can go back to hanging out among underwater plants, looking like nothing more than a dead leaf.

A water bug needs to breathe air, which it gets by swimming to the water's surface and sticking a tube on its backside out of the water. It can also store bubbles of air under its wings for breathing.

The bug's hind legs are also adaptations for a life underwater. They are flattened and lined with hairlike bristles, which makes them good paddles for swimming. These bugs also have wings and can fly. They usually fly during late spring and early summer to seek mates and may fly to new ponds to find one.

This giant water bug is a different species called *Lethocerus indicus*. It's big enough to cover the palm of your hand! People eat this big bug in some parts of Asia.

A giant water bug is big enough to catch a small frog. Even bigger water bugs can be found in parts of South America—some are up to four inches (10 cm) long! These big bugs have been known to catch baby turtles, birds, and even small snakes.

233

ASIAN GIANT HORNET

FACTS

FAMILY Vespidae

OTHER COMMON NAMES
Yak-killer

SCIENTIFIC NAME
Vespa mandarinia

SIZE 1.4 to 2.2 inches
(3.5 to 5.5 cm)

FOOD Insects, tree sap, fruit

HABITAT Forested areas

RANGE Eastern and
southeastern Asia, north of
tropical regions

Meet the world's biggest hornet! Or—not.

This isn't a hornet you want to get anywhere near.

The queen is the largest insect in a colony of Asian giant hornets. She can be up to 2.2 inches (5.5 cm) long. The workers are a bit smaller, but they're equipped with a stinger up to 0.2 inch (6 mm) long. That's about half as long as the point on an ordinary pushpin.

The hornets use their stings to protect their queen and nest from predators. The nest is built in soil, among tree roots, in old rodent burrows, or in hollow trees. The queen stays in the nest to lay eggs and is fed and cared for by workers.

Workers also feed the larvae after they hatch. They catch insects, kill them with their mandibles, and chew them up to make giant-hornet baby food. A worker can't digest solid food, but when it feeds this mush to a larva, it gets back a few swallows of nutritious spit from the larva's mouth. Yuk!

These hornets are known to stage raids on bee nests and beehives to feed their young. At first, a few hornets sit outside a bee nest. They catch a few bees and bring them back home. Then a hornet marks the nest with a smell that alerts other workers to attack it. Hornets pour into the nest and kill all the bees in battles that can last for hours. Then the hornets take over the nest and live in it until they have fed all the bees' larvae and pupae to the wasp larvae.

An Asian giant hornet's wingspan can be up to three inches (7.6 cm) wide—almost as wide as the wingspan of the smallest bird, the bee hummingbird.

A single Asian giant hornet can kill 40 bees in just one minute with its mandibles.

The tarantula hawk wasp isn't interested in stinging people, but she will sting if she is bothered. The pain of the sting is rated as one of the most painful insect stings in the world.

TARANTULA HAWK WASP

Tarantulas are supersize spiders. Some species are bigger than a human hand. But if tarantulas had nightmares, they would probably be about tarantula hawk wasps.

Just like its prey, the tarantula hawk wasp is supersize. A female can be up to two inches (5.1 cm) long. She is also equipped with a stinger—her only weapon against the tarantula's size, jaws, and venomous fangs.

When a female wasp finds a tarantula burrow, she snips and tugs at the pad of silk strung across its entrance. She may then enter the burrow, or the tarantula may come charging out.

That's when the battle begins. The wasp moves quickly to avoid the tarantula's fangs. She darts in and out and wrestles with the spider as she tries to sting it. Finally, she jabs her stinger into one of the weak spots on the tarantula's tough exoskeleton— the place where a leg joins to the body. The venom works instantly. The tarantula is now completely paralyzed, but it isn't dead.

But the wasp doesn't eat its prey. Instead, she drags it back into the tarantula's burrow or into one she dug herself. Then she lays an egg on its abdomen. Finally, she buries it and flies off to find another tarantula.

The still living tarantula is food for the larva that hatches from the egg. As it grows, the larva will eat its entombed meal.

FACTS

FAMILY Pompilidae

OTHER COMMON NAMES Tarantula wasp

SCIENTIFIC NAME *Pepsis grossa*

SIZE 0.9 to 2 inches (2.4 to 5.1 cm)

FOOD Nectar, pollen

HABITAT Desert scrublands

RANGE Southwestern and central United States, Mexico, Central America, northern South America

Some tarantula hawk wasps have black wings. Others have orange wings. The two different forms are rarely found living in the same places.

ANT LION LARVA

FACTS

FAMILY Myrmeleontidae

OTHER COMMON NAMES
Doodlebug

SCIENTIFIC NAME
Myrmeleon spp.

SIZE 0.5 inch (1.3 cm)

FOOD Ants and other small insects, spiders

HABITAT Sandy soil

RANGE Worldwide

Female ant lions lay their eggs in sandy or dusty soil that is just right for the larvae's pit-making purposes.

A baby that piles sand on its head and can only walk backward doesn't sound like much of a predator. And it's not—unless you're an ant.

This "baby" is the young, or larva, of some species of the ant lion. In fact, the insect gets its name from its larval stage, because the adult ant lion isn't lionlike at all. It is a graceful insect that only feeds on nectar and pollen. The larva, however, is a barrel-shaped creature with curved jaws.

The larva eats insects, mainly ants. It catches them using that favorite predator trick of sit-and-wait, but with a twist. First, it uses its back end to dig up sand. Sand piles up on its head, which is shaped a little like a shovel. Then it flips the little pile of sand out of the pit with a jerk of its head and jaws. It keeps backing up, digging, and flipping until it has dug a funnel-shaped pit. Finally, it buries itself in the middle of the pit ... and waits.

The pit is only up to two inches (5 cm) deep, but that's enough to trap an ant. Any ant that stumbles into the pit can't easily get out. It can't get a grip. The only grip belongs to the jaws of the ant lion, which bursts out of its hole to grab the ant. Its bristles help fasten the ant lion in place. If the ant lion does lose its grip, it will toss sand up the sides of its pit to make them even more slippery and force the ant to slide down toward it.

Then the ant lion sinks its jaws into the ant. Digestive juices flow into the ant's body, turning its insides into mush that the ant lion can slurp up. Next it flicks the ant's body out of the pit and buries itself to wait for its next victim.

An ant lion can spend as long as
three years as a larva. During
that entire time, it doesn't go to
the bathroom—all its waste is
stored in its body. Yuk!

A female magnificent spider makes egg cases that are bigger than she is. Each one can contain about 600 eggs. Her mate, however, is less than one-tenth her size!

MAGNIFICENT SPIDER

Spiders have all sorts of clever ways of catching a meal. Some species build sticky webs. Others lurk in flowers or stalk and jump on prey. There's one group of spiders, however, that has really come up with an amazing behavior: It makes a tool out of silk to "fish" for moths.

These spiders are called the bolas spiders. A bolas is a traditional hunting tool used in South America to catch animals. It consists of a set of weights that are connected by cords. They are whirled around and thrown at a running animal to catch it by tangling up its legs.

A bolas spider's "bolas" is a silken cord that has a blob of sticky silk at its tip. Only the female spider makes this device. She also has sensitive bristles on her legs that can detect the wingbeats of moths coming close. When the spider senses that the moth is in striking range, she whirls the cord and flings it. The moth is then caught on the sticky blob.

The magnificent spider is a kind of bolas spider found in Australia. (Other species of bolas spider live in Africa and the Americas.) The female spider gives off scents at night that attract prey. The scent is a chemical, called a pheromone, that is like the scent given off by different species of female moths. It lures male moths, which follow the scent hoping to find mates—but are snared by the tricky spider instead.

Another species found in America called *Mastophora hutchinsoni* attracts different kinds of moths at different times of night. The spider gives off one scent when one kind of moth is active and then switches to the second scent when another moth species starts fluttering about at a later time.

FACTS

FAMILY Araneidae

OTHER COMMON NAMES
Bolas spider, bola spider

SCIENTIFIC NAME
Ordgarius magnificus

SIZE .08 to 0.6 inch (2 to 14 mm)

FOOD Moths

HABITAT Forests, parks, gardens

RANGE Eastern Australia

Bolas spiders hunt at night. By day, they sleep hidden among leaves. Many species of bolas spiders, such as *Mastophora cornigera*, also wear colors and patterns that make them look like a glob of bird poop so they can hide in plain sight.

This female goldenrod crab spider blends in with the daisy's petals. Her camouflage helps her snag meals like this fly. That meal, by the way, is bigger than a male goldenrod crab spider! The male is a tiny brown-and-white creature that looks as if he's a totally different species.

GOLDENROD CRAB SPIDER

The goldenrod crab spider is one of more than 2,000 species of crab spiders worldwide. It's named for the bright yellow color that the female spider often wears. But she isn't always yellow—she can also turn white or pale green over the span of a few days or weeks. This color change helps her match the flowers on which she sits.

Crab spiders perch on flowers because that's where their prey feeds. Like a lioness at a water hole, the spider waits for a bee or other insect to stop for a drink. She watches for any sign of motion with her two rows of eyes. She waits with her two pairs of extra-long front legs spread wide, ready to pinch prey.

Once the spider has her prey, she bites it to inject venom. Her digestive fluids turn it into "bug juice" that she can then slurp up.

She needs all the food she can get, because she needs to produce eggs. The eggs are stowed in a cup made of a folded-over leaf tip and wrapped in silk made by glands in her body. She guards the eggs until she dies at the start of winter.

Next time you're around a patch of daisies, goldenrod, or other white or yellow flowers, look closely to see if you can find this spider hiding among them. A bee or butterfly curled up in a weird position on a flower and not moving may also be a clue that this little predator is at work.

FACTS

FAMILY Thomisidae

OTHER COMMON NAMES Red-spotted crab spider, flower spider

SCIENTIFIC NAME *Misumena vatia*

SIZE .12 to .35 inch (3 to 9 mm)

FOOD Bees, wasps, butterflies, flies, and other insects that visit flowers

HABITAT Grasslands, meadows, gardens, parks, wetlands

RANGE North America, Europe

Crab spiders don't make webs, but they make silk not only for egg sacs but also for "droplines" they can use to drop from a leaf or flower to another location.

A tarantula's fangs curve down and tuck under its body when not in use. The spider jabs downward to sink its fangs into prey.

GOLIATH BIRDEATER

The goliath birdeater is a species of tarantula that is the heaviest spider in the world. It weighs up to six ounces (170 grams—about as much as five or six house mice).

A house mouse, by the way, is a prey item that this spider can easily tackle—it's certainly big enough. Its size is what puts the word "goliath" in its name. But the "birdeater" part is a bit misleading. Though a goliath birdeater can catch a small bird, such as a hummingbird, it rarely does. Its main meals are insects and other spiders.

Like other tarantulas, the goliath birdeater makes its home in a burrow. This burrow is lined with silk made by the spider. Silken lines stretch out of the burrow. These lines are trip wires that detect prey passing by. When the spider feels the lines tremble, it rushes out of its burrow to grab the passerby.

That prey is quickly subdued by this spider's venom, which is delivered by fangs that can measure nearly an inch (2.5 cm) long! Though prey can't survive the birdeater's venom, the venom doesn't do much harm to predators that attack the birdeater.

So instead of using its fangs to defend itself against attackers, the birdeater relies on its bristles. These bristles are called urticating hairs. "Urticating" is a fancy word for "irritating." If you've ever been stung by a plant such as a nettle, you've felt the sting of urticating hairs.

The irritating bristles sit on the tarantula's abdomen. If it's disturbed, it brushes the bristles off its abdomen with two of its hind legs. The bristles have barbs on them that irritate the sensitive skin of the attacker's eyes and nostrils.

FACTS

FAMILY Theraphosidae

OTHER COMMON NAMES
Goliath bird-eating spider

SCIENTIFIC NAME
Theraphosa blondi

SIZE Body, 3 inches (7.5 cm); leg span, 11 inches (28 cm)

FOOD Insects, spiders, earthworms, small reptiles, mice

HABITAT Rain forests

RANGE Northern South America

The giant huntsman spider has legs that span up to 12 inches (30 cm), which makes it just a bit bigger than a goliath birdeater. The birdeater, however, is heavier and bulkier.

245

A sea spider's body is so small that its digestive system actually stretches into its legs. There isn't enough room in its abdomen to fit it all. The pumping motion that pushes food through the digestive system in the legs also helps to keep freshly oxygenated blood flowing through the spider.

GIANT SEA SPIDER

The giant sea spider isn't actually a spider, though it belongs to the same group as spiders: arthropods. An arthropod is an invertebrate with a tough exoskeleton that forms a jointed coat of armor. Insects, spiders, crabs, lobsters, and centipedes are other examples of arthropods.

There are around 1,300 known species of sea spiders. They range in size from tiny, short-legged animals less than 0.1 inch (3 mm) wide to creatures as large as this giant sea spider, which walks on spindly legs that span up to 27.5 inches (70 cm) in length. These legs are connected to a very small abdomen.

Up front is a long snout called a proboscis. A sea spider eats by sticking its proboscis into its prey and slurping up the contents of its body. This adaptation—imagine getting all your food by sucking it up with a straw—requires that it prey only on soft-bodied animals.

Luckily for a sea spider, the ocean offers many soft-bodied animals to eat! Its prey is often a cnidarian, such as a coral or a sea anemone. They also feast on sponges, marine worms called polychaetes, and mossy-looking, coral-like creatures called bryozoans.

The giant sea spider, like other large sea spiders, lives in deep, cold water. Some scientists think sea spiders grow extra large at Earth's poles because their bodies' functions work so slowly at near-freezing temperatures that they don't need much oxygen to survive. However, their cold habitat is very rich in oxygen. As a result, they can easily grow large as they quietly live life in the very slow lane.

FACTS

FAMILY Colossendeidae

OTHER COMMON NAMES None

SCIENTIFIC NAME *Colossendeis megalonyx*

SIZE 0.8 inch (2 cm), not including legs

FOOD Soft corals, hydrozoans

HABITAT Sandy seafloors

RANGE Antarctic and subantarctic waters; also found below 9,840 feet (3,000 m) in parts of Indian and South Pacific Oceans

Tiny marine arthropods sometimes hitch rides on the long legs of big sea spiders.

There are more than 1,500 known species of scorpions, but only a few species—about 50 of them—have venom that is strong enough to seriously harm a person.

EMPEROR SCORPION

Like spiders, scorpions are arachnids with eight legs. A scorpion also has a pair of pincers. But the first thing people may think of when they hear "scorpion" is the stinger at the tip of its hind end.

A scorpion's stinger is a sharp spine that delivers venom made in glands in its abdomen. Many species use the stinger to kill prey, and all of them use their stingers to defend themselves from predators. To sting another animal, a scorpion curls its back end over its body so it looks like a walking letter C. Then it jabs its stinger forward, again and again.

Scorpions are active at night. Some species hunt for prey, while many species sit at the mouths of their burrows to ambush prey that stroll by. Scorpions don't have good eyesight, but their bodies are covered with bristles that are very sensitive to vibrations. They can sense the motion of small animals nearby. A scorpion can even use this sense of touch to grab a flying insect out of the air.

One of the largest species is the emperor scorpion. It uses venom to kill prey when it is young and small, but by the time it's an adult, it uses its strong pincers instead. It takes a lot of energy to make venom, after all, and saving energy is an adaptation that helps animals survive. The emperor scorpion simply mashes its prey into a pulp that is sloshed with digestive juices so it can slurp it up with its tiny mouth.

Emperor scorpions are big enough to kill mice, but termites are their main prey. They often live in burrows that are right inside termite mounds, so food is literally on their doorstep.

FACTS

FAMILY Scorpionidae

OTHER COMMON NAMES
Emperor black scorpion, imperial scorpion

SCIENTIFIC NAME
Pandinus imperator

SIZE 8 inches (20 cm)

FOOD Worms, insects, mice, lizards

HABITAT Rain forests, savannas

RANGE Western Africa

A female emperor scorpion gives birth to tiny, white mini versions of herself. They all clamber up on her back and stay there for a few days or so, until they're able to hunt on their own. Mom guards them fiercely while they're on her back, but after that, the babies better watch out. She won't recognize them as her own and will readily eat them.

GIANT CENTIPEDE

FACTS

FAMILY Scolopendridae

OTHER COMMON NAMES Amazonian giant centipede, Peruvian giant yellow-leg centipede

SCIENTIFIC NAME *Scolopendra gigantea*

SIZE Up to 12 inches (30 cm)

FOOD Mice, bats, lizards, frogs, toads, insects, spiders, snails, worms

HABITAT Tropical and subtropical forests

RANGE Northern South America, various Caribbean islands

A grasshopper mouse makes a meal for a giant centipede. But sometimes the tables are turned. Grasshopper mice move fast and can dodge the centipede's fangs. They even eat centipedes themselves.

Centipedes have long bodies made up of body segments. Each segment has a pair of legs. These animals range greatly in size. Some species are so small, they're barely visible. Many are an inch or two (2.5 to 5 cm) long. And then there's the centipede that's as big as a ruler.

This oversize arthropod is the giant centipede. It scuttles across forest floors on 21 to 23 pairs of legs. Like other centipedes, it has a special pair of claws just behind its mouth for killing prey. These claws contain venom, which is injected into prey to kill it. A giant centipede is hefty enough to attack prey that's as big as a mouse or even a small rat.

Scientists studying giant centipedes in Venezuela made an amazing discovery in 2000. They were exploring a cave when they spotted a giant centipede on the ceiling, munching on a bat! Over the next few years, they found more centipedes eating bats. But how did they catch them?

The centipedes caught the bats by hanging upside down from the cave ceiling and grabbing them as they flew by. A captured bat was immediately bitten near its head so that it died quickly. Then the centipede held it with many pairs of its front legs while clinging to the ceiling with legs near its hind end.

Few animals are willing to tackle a giant centipede. However, the little Caribbean scorpion *Centruroides testaceus* is. You'd need to line up about six of these scorpions to equal the length of a giant centipede. This scorpion usually preys on insects and spiders, but it will attack a female centipede that's coiled around her eggs in a burrow. While the centipede is in this vulnerable position, the scorpion is able to inject her with its deadly venom.

A giant centipede has antennae on its head. It also has two legs on its hind end that have evolved to sense things such as food, too.

EUNICID WORM

FACTS

FAMILY Eunicidae

OTHER COMMON NAMES
Rock worm, bristle worm

SCIENTIFIC NAME *Eunice* spp.

SIZE Up to 10 feet (3 m)

FOOD Fish, worms, and other small prey; carrion; seaweed and other algae

HABITAT Warm ocean waters

RANGE Worldwide

In 2009, scientists found a *Eunice aphroditois* worm that had been living in a wooden float in an outdoor fish pen. It measured 9.8 feet (3 m) long and weighed 15.3 ounces (433 g)—about the weight of four sticks of butter.

Those earthworms wriggling around in your backyard or local park have very distant cousins in the ocean. These marine worms are known as polychaetes or bristle worms. There are more than 10,000 known species, and the Eunicid worms are just one group among many. It contains more than 200 species, which include a few that grow to enormous lengths.

One of the biggest species is *Eunice aphroditois*. It can be up to 10 feet (3 m) long! It embeds most of its length in the seafloor, where it waits for fish, worms, and other prey to swim over its hiding place. Its head is equipped with antenna-like body parts that can sense changes in light and chemistry in the water above it. The antennae may also function as lures to attract fish.

When the worm detects prey—*wham!* It bolts up from the seafloor. It has several sets of jaws that spring from its throat and snap at the prey, which may be cut in half by the impact. Prey is then dragged into the worm's burrow.

Like most other bristle worms, worms in this family have little limbs covered with bristles sticking out of their body segments. These limbs take different forms in different species of bristle worms—they can be fins for swimming, scoops for digging, or legs for creeping. They help that superlong *Eunice aphroditois* get a grip on the sides of its seafloor burrow.

Different kinds of Eunicid worms may live in burrows or simply find shelter in cracks and other hidey-holes among rocks or coral reefs.

Little fish called monocle breams sometimes "mob" a *Eunice aphroditois* worm and blow jets of water at it until it pulls its body back into its burrow. Being mobbed like this spoils the worm's ability to launch a sneaky surprise attack.

MORE ABOUT
PREDATORS

TIBETAN FOX
Vulpes ferrilata

The Tibetan fox is found in grasslands and near deserts in parts of China, Nepal, India, and neighboring countries. It feeds on hares, rodents, and other small animals, but its main prey are little rabbit-like creatures called pikas. Tibetan foxes can dig up pikas hiding in burrows, but they will also tag after brown bears to snag an easy meal: If the bear digs up pika burrows, the fox can grab any pikas that try to escape from the bear.

BELUGA WHALE
Delphinapterus leucas

Moo! Chirp! Click! Sounds like these are made by beluga whales as they "chat" with members of their group. These small white whales eat dozens of different kinds of prey: fish, shrimps, crabs, mussels, clams, snails, sandworms, squid, octopuses ... the list goes on! Belugas find their prey in shallow waters of the Arctic Ocean and its seas. In turn, belugas are sometimes caught by polar bears.

FISHING CAT
Prionailurus viverrinus

A fishing cat has an otter-like head and partly webbed front feet. It hunts for fish in rivers, lakes, ponds, and wetlands in parts of Southeast Asia, snagging prey with its long claws or grabbing it with its teeth. Beneath the long hair of its outer fur coat lies a layer of short, thick fur that keeps it dry in water. Fishing cats can also hunt on land, where they catch and eat everything from frogs to sheep.

NORTHERN PIKE
Esox lucius

Northern pike are freshwater fish that are widespread in Earth's northern hemisphere. These fierce predators eat almost anything they can catch, from fish and frogs to ducklings and mice. A pike can swallow prey that's half as long as it is! Many pike hunt by hiding among water plants and ambushing prey that comes by. Prey is seized by a pike's sharp teeth, which point backward in its mouth.

HARRIS'S HAWK
Parabuteo unicinctus

Harris's hawks soar over dry lands in the southwestern United States as well as parts of Central and South America. They're famous for hunting as a team. A group of hawks may take turns chasing a rabbit or rodent until it's completely worn out and easy to catch. A hawk may also scare prey out of its hiding place—straight into the talons and beaks of one of its teammates (see p. 17).

EPOMIS BEETLE
Epomis circumscriptus

Frogs, toads, and salamanders eat insects—but they better not mess with Epomis beetles! These insects have evolved to prey on amphibians. Adult beetles attack by biting their prey on the back. An Epomis larva, like the one pictured, however, wiggles its antennae to get a frog to attack it. Then the larva jams its sharp jaws into the frog. It clings tightly and starts feeding—first by sucking up the body fluids of its prey and then by chewing it down to the bones.

A TALK WITH
ADRIAN TREVES

A SCIENTIST DEDICATED TO CARNIVORE CONSERVATION

Adrian Treves is a conservation biologist and professor of environmental studies at the University of Wisconsin–Madison. In 2007, he set up the Carnivore Coexistence Lab (CCL) at the school. The CCL is devoted to the study of large carnivores such as wolves and lions. We spoke with Adrian to learn about what he does and how scientists work.

What does a conservation biologist do?

A conservation biologist works to understand nature and preserve it for future generations. The "biologist" part means we focus on wild, living creatures in nature. The "conservation" part means we try to balance humans' need for nature (for example, for fishing or clearing wild habitat to grow crops) with other living things' need for food, shelter, and space to live and reproduce.

Tell us more about what you do.

I focus on preserving large carnivores, such as wolves, bears, and big cats, so that none of them go extinct and so future generations can enjoy all the benefits of sharing Earth with them. To do that, I teach students and the public. I persuade governments and other decision-makers to understand what are effective methods for coexistence with carnivores—that means living near them. We know far less than we think we do about these carnivores and even about the people who coexist with them, so I spend a lot of time and effort researching the ecology of carnivores. (Ecology is the study of the relationships between living things and their physical environment.)

What inspired you to become a scientist?

As a kid, I loved animals and being outdoors. As a college student, I wanted to unravel the mysteries of evolution and ecology. I completed many years of school and training in many countries (11 of them!) before I became a professor of conservation biology. As a conservation biologist, I believe deeply that we owe it to our children and their children to preserve this Earth and leave its creatures unimpaired.

Why did you choose to study predators?

I've long been fascinated with how prey animals avoid danger and protect themselves. Predators have to overcome each of their prey's defenses, and I find it amazing how predators and their prey solve those perpetual challenges. That's not just an intriguing question—it also has many everyday applications.

For example, how do farmers protect livestock from predators, whether those predators are wolves or free-ranging dogs? How do we manage competition between human hunters who are predators that want deer to eat, and wild predators that naturally prey on deer?

What's your favorite predatory species?

Sometimes wolves are my favorite because they form loving family units that we call "packs," and their packs are so cooperative. But sometimes my favorite is the leopard.

Male lion feasting on a giraffe carcass in Ndutu, Tanzania, photographed by Adrian Treves

Leopards are solitary foragers and rarely associate with other leopards. Their beautiful spotted coats and stealth make them fantastic to me.

What do you find most fascinating about predators?

Humans have fear and awe of predators, especially the larger ones, so we react to them in unpredictable ways. For example, many people give predators human traits such as "good" and "evil." But predators are just acting the way evolution shaped them. So I am fascinated by the challenges of preserving predators in nature, despite the intolerance of many humans toward them.

What is the most awesome experience you've had as a conservation biologist?

I'd say the times I've been alone in the forest and seen a rare wild animal going about its daily life. I once saw a jaguarundi in Belize when I was sitting still in the forest. The jaguarundi is a wild cat with a long, slinky body and a tail that helps it climb. I watched it climb a tree right near some monkeys I was studying. Both the monkeys and I were caught off guard by this amazing cat.

I didn't know jaguarundis were in that Central American region and had never seen one before (or since!), so the mystery and surprise cemented the memory for me. Every time I see a wild predator in the flesh, I feel that thrill again because wild predators are shy of people, and dwindling in numbers almost everywhere in the world.

What do you think is the best approach to the issues surrounding predators and livestock? (That is, how is it best to achieve carnivore coexistence?)

First, we need to believe that coexistence is better than eradication—that is, getting rid of predators. There are many reasons to favor coexistence. It's better for the benefit of future generations; it's better for the wild predators; and it's better for our ecosystems on which all life depends.

Second, we need to let scientific evidence guide us about which methods work to protect livestock without harming wild predators—not fear and tradition, which are not reliable guides. We should use scientific evidence to decide what are effective methods for coexistence. *Then* people can argue about which methods fit our needs best, case by case.

Finally, we need to stop fighting among ourselves about who gets the power to decide who owns wildlife. We are just temporary guardians of life on this planet. These wild animals belong to all of us and to future people.

What should we know about predators to help us understand why they are so important?

Without predators, the ecosystems we depend on would fall apart. We would lose the plants and animals we love, which depend on healthy predator populations. Future generations will thank us for preserving nature instead of destroying it.

What advice would you give kids who want to study wildlife?

Find something that helps others and makes the world a better place. Read everything that comes your way, especially books and articles by experts. There's a lot of "noise" in our popular culture, but you can learn to ignore the noise and pick out the music that makes you feel better about yourself and the world around you. Work hard every day at that one thing, and excel at it!

Lioness, with an injured left front paw, and her cubs in the Serengeti of Tanzania, photographed by Adrian Treves

257

HOW YOU CAN HELP

According to the World Wide Fund for Nature's 2016 Living Planet Report, there has been a steep decline in numbers of vertebrates (animals with backbones) since 1970. The report states that studies of more than 3,500 different species of fish, mammals, birds, reptiles, and amphibians worldwide show that their populations have dropped by 58 percent. This situation will only get worse if nations fail to do anything to stop the decline. What can you do to help turn the situation around?

CURB GLOBAL CLIMATE CHANGE

According to scientists, burning fossil fuels, such as oil and gasoline, releases heat-trapping gases into the atmosphere. The result is global climate change—a change in Earth's climate. This phenomenon threatens Earth and its life—and humans—in many ways.

It may seem as if this is too big a problem for an ordinary person to tackle, but every bit of effort helps. You can help reduce the burning of fossil fuels by turning off lights when you leave a room, replacing traditional lightbulbs with LED (light-emitting diode) bulbs or fluorescent ones, putting on a sweatshirt instead of turning up the heat, drying clothes on a clothesline instead of in the dryer, and getting to school by walking, biking, riding a bus, or joining a carpool. This effort is called "reducing your carbon footprint."

REDUCE, REUSE, RECYCLE

Recycling an aluminum can, drinking from a reusable container, or bringing a reusable bag to the grocery store don't sound like activities that can help lions, wolves, and other predators. But these everyday choices are small actions that can add up to make a big impact. Take that aluminum can, for example: It can be melted down and used to make new cans using just a fraction of the energy it takes to dig up and refine a new batch of aluminum. Saving energy and materials helps protect habitats, too, because it slows down the rate at which we humans dig and drill in those habitats. Finally, it also means less fossil fuel is burned and fewer greenhouse gases are sent into the sea and sky to contribute to global climate change.

JOIN AN ORGANIZATION OR PROJECT

Check with a local nature center or science museum to see if it has a club or project focusing on wildlife. There are also projects you can find online that seek data from near and far from "citizen scientists"—people who are interested in learning about science and observing the natural world. Many of these projects welcome participation by kids. For example, the Lost Ladybug Project uses information gathered by citizen scientists to find out about native species of ladybugs in the United States and track changes in their distribution and population. These little predators gobble up aphids and other pests found on garden plants. Find out more at lostladybug.org. You can also record observations of raptors and other birds you see online at eBird, which is a project of the Audubon Society and the Cornell Lab of Ornithology. Find out more at ebird.org/about.

PICK UP THE TRASH

Help keep your neighborhood, parks, and beaches clean. Put on a pair of gloves to pick up trash. You can also help cut down on litter at its source by buying fewer products that use a lot of packaging. For example, you can buy fruit that's sold loose in bins instead of in plastic packaging.

In addition, when you take out the garbage, make sure the bags don't stick out of the bin and attract animals. If you live in an area where there are coyotes and bears, it might be best to ask if the bins can be stored in the garage. These predators and others have learned that human neighborhoods are filled with food to scavenge and even pets and backyard chickens to eat. Predators that get too familiar with people lose their fear of them, which puts the animals in danger of being removed or even killed by authorities who fear they will one day harm people.

USE FEWER PLASTIC PRODUCTS

Plastics that end up as ocean debris entangle, drown, and kill tens of thousands of marine animals each year, including predators such as seals and sea lions. On land, predators that scavenge can get their heads stuck in plastic containers or even swallow harmful objects. Consider taking a reusable cloth bag to the grocery store instead of taking home plastic bags. By cutting down on plastics, you'll also help to curb global climate change.

KEEP YOUR CAT INSIDE AND YOUR DOG ON A LEASH

Cats that are allowed to wander outside not only kill millions of birds each year but also become prey for wild animals such as coyotes. This can lead to persecution of coyotes and other wild animals because pet owners blame the predators for the loss of their pets. As for dogs, they're often tempted to chase wild animals—like cats, which are predators! They may harm wildlife that are prey animals, or have a nasty run-in with a wild predator and get injured themselves.

KEEP LEARNING—AND SHARING!

Keep on reading about wild animals and finding out all you can about them (see Find Out More, p. 262). You can also help other people learn to love and cherish the world's wildlife—including predators—simply by sharing the wonder of these amazing creatures.

A good way to learn about predators is to find organizations devoted to a particular species. For example, the Snow Leopard Trust (snowleopard.org) is devoted to conserving snow leopards and their habitat. The Peregrine Fund (peregrinefund.org) works to conserve peregrine falcons and other birds of prey and to educate people about these predators. You can also share your wildlife images and observations with other people, including scientists, at inaturalist.org, a project associated with the California Academy of Sciences.

GLOSSARY

ADAPTATION — a feature that helps a living organism survive in its environment

AMBUSH PREDATION — a predatory behavior that involves sitting in one place or hiding and then attacking prey that happens to come close

CACHING — storing food for later in a way that hides or protects it from other animals

CAMOUFLAGE — an organism's ability to disguise its appearance, often by using its coloring or body shape to blend in with its surroundings. An example is an insect that looks like a leaf.

CANID — a mammal that is in the dog family, Canidae

CARCASS — the body of a dead animal

CARNASSIAL TEETH — pairs of teeth in the sides of a carnivore's upper and lower jaw that move past each other like scissors to slice meat

CARNIVORE — specifically, a mammal that belongs to a group called Carnivora; generally, an animal that eats meat

CARRION — the decaying flesh of a dead animal

CLIMATE — the kinds of weather conditions that are normal for a large area over the span of many years

CLIMATE CHANGE — a big change in Earth's climate that lasts for a very long time. For example, Earth has periodically experienced ice ages, when large areas of its lands have been covered by ice sheets.

CNIDARIAN — an invertebrate animal with a sacklike body and stinging cells that lives in water and is part of a large group, or phylum, called Cnidaria. This group includes animals such as corals and jellyfish.

CONSERVATION — protecting wildlife and habitats and using resources carefully and wisely so as to preserve them for the future

DECOMPOSE — to break down or decay

ECOSYSTEM — a community of living things interacting with each other and the nonliving parts of their environment

ELASMOBRANCHS — the group of fish that includes sharks, rays, and skates

ENVIRONMENT — the natural features of a place, such as its weather, the kind of land it has, and the type of plants that grow in it

EVOLUTION — the process of genetic change over time. Living things change genetically, or evolve, over millions of years. These changes are called adaptations and help animals survive in habitats, which also can change over time.

FELID — a mammal that is in the cat family, Felidae

FLADRY — flapping pieces of plastic or other materials used to keep predators away from livestock

GENETIC — having to do with an organism's genes, the pieces of DNA in cells that tell them how to make proteins. These proteins control or influence the traits that a living thing inherits from its parents.

GRASSLANDS — lands that are covered by grasses. Prairies and savannas are examples of grasslands.

GREENHOUSE GAS — a gas in the atmosphere that traps heat. Carbon dioxide, water vapor, methane, and nitrous oxide are examples of greenhouse gases.

GUILD — a group of living things that all use the same resources. For example, wolves and coyotes eat the same prey and so they are in the same guild.

HABITAT — a place in nature where an organism lives throughout the year, or for shorter periods of time

HERBIVORE — an animal that only eats plants

INSECTIVORE — an animal that feeds mainly or only on insects

INTRAGUILD PREDATION — predation by a predator on another predator within its guild; for example, a wolf killing a coyote

INVASIVE SPECIES — species that are introduced accidentally or on purpose from their native habitat to a new location. Invasive species have a bad effect on native plants and animals.

INVERTEBRATE — an organism without a backbone. Invertebrates include insects, corals, crustaceans, and spiders.

LARVA (PLURAL: LARVAE) — an immature form of an invertebrate animal, such as an insect

OMNIVORE — an animal that eats both plants and animals

PREDATOR — an animal that kills and eats other animals

PREDATORY — relating to an animal that kills or behavior that involves killing

PREY — any animal that is hunted and eaten by other animals

RAIN FOREST — a forest with upward of 160 inches (406 cm) of rain in a year

RAPTOR — a bird with keen eyesight and a hooked beak that catches prey with its feet. Owls and hawks are examples of raptors.

SCAVENGER — an animal that eats carrion (dead organisms)

SCRUBLANDS — lands that are mainly covered by bushes

SPECIES — a group of organisms that share similar traits and are able to breed with each other to produce living young

STALKING PREDATION — a predatory behavior that involves sneaking up on prey and then attacking it

SUBANTARCTIC — describes parts of Earth that lie just outside Antarctic regions

SUBARCTIC — describes parts of Earth that lie just outside Arctic regions

TALON — the claw of a raptor

VENOM — a toxic substance produced by an animal's body and injected into other animals by biting or stinging. A venomous reptile is one that produces venom.

VERTEBRATE — an organism with a backbone. Vertebrates include amphibians, birds, fish, mammals, and reptiles.

WETLANDS — areas where water covers the soil or is near its surface for some or all of the year. Marshes, swamps, and bogs are examples of wetlands.

FIND OUT
MORE

WEBSITES

Plenty of pictures and animal facts can be found about predators and prey alike at the National Geographic Kids "Animals" website: natgeokids.com/animals

The San Diego Zoo's website includes general information about animals and also in-depth sections about different species: kids .sandiegozoo.org/animals

Check out mammals, reptiles, insects, and more at the University of Michigan's BioKids website, where you can find a Critter Catalog: biokids.umich.edu/critters/

Plug in the name of an animal to find out more at the Smithsonian's National Zoo and Conservation Biology Institute website: nationalzoo .si.edu/animals/list

Find out more about bats at Bat Conservation International's site: batcon.org/resources/ media-education/learning

Reptiles, raptors, and more await you at the Bronx Zoo's website: bronxzoo.com/exhibits

Sharks and other predators of the watery world swim at the National Aquarium. Visit them at their website: aqua.org/ explore/animals

Find out more about owls, hawks, eagles, and other raptors on the website of the World Center for Birds of Prey: peregrinefund.org/visit

MOVIES
BBC

- *Extreme Bears* (2014): Explore the life of grizzlies and other bears in their natural habitats.

- *The Hunt* (2016): This series reveals the challenges faced by predators of many kinds, from insects to whales.

- *Shark: The Ocean's Greatest Predators* (2015): Great whites, blacktips, wobbegongs, and more! A close-up look at the ocean's apex predators.

National Geographic

- *Hidden World of the Bengal Tiger* (2010): See how a female tiger survives and raises her young.

- *Lions of the African Night* (2016): Intrepid filmmakers reveal what lions are up to after the sun sets and they go hunting.

- *National Geographic Classics: Super Predators* (2014): This collection features animals ranging from tigers and vipers to orcas.

- *National Geographic Classics: World's Deadliest* (2011): This collection focuses on predators including lions, crocodiles, king cobras, bears, sharks, and spiders.

- *Secret Life of Predators* (2013): This documentary explores the lives of predators on land and in the ocean.

Nature

- *American Eagle* (2016): Soar with North America's amazing bald eagle.

- *Cold Warriors: Wolves and Buffalo* (2013): Watch the ancient drama of predator and prey unfold between bison and wolf in Wood Buffalo National Park.

- *Magic of the Snowy Owl* (2012): Find out about the white, winged hunter of the snowy Arctic.

- *Wolverine: Chasing the Phantom* (2011): What do we know about this mysterious mammal of the Far North?

PLACES TO VISIT

U.S.A.

- **Bronx Zoo,** Bronx, New York: *bronxzoo.com*

- **Brookfield Zoo,** Chicago, Illinois: *czs.org/brookfield-zoo/plan-your-visit/information*

- **Cincinnati Zoo,** Cincinnati, Ohio: *cincinnatizoo.org*

- **Columbus Zoo,** Columbus, Ohio: *columbuszoo.org*

- **Dallas Zoo,** Dallas, Texas: *dallaszoo.com*

- **Denver Zoo,** Denver, Colorado: *denverzoo.org*

- **Henry Doorly Zoo,** Omaha, Nebraska: *omahazoo.com*

- **Houston Zoo,** Houston, Texas: *houstonzoo.org*

- **Lincoln Park Zoo,** Chicago, Illinois: *lpzoo.org*

- **Memphis Zoo,** Memphis, Tennessee: *memphiszoo.org*

- **North Carolina Zoo,** Asheboro, North Carolina: *nczoo.org*

- **Oregon Zoo,** Portland, Oregon: *oregonzoo.org*

- **Philadelphia Zoo,** Philadelphia, Pennsylvania: *philadelphiazoo.org*

- **San Diego Zoo,** San Diego, California: *zoo.sandiegozoo.org*

- **Smithsonian National Zoological Park,** Washington, D.C.: *nationalzoo.si.edu*

- **St. Louis Zoo,** St. Louis, Missouri: *stlzoo.org*

- **Woodland Park Zoo,** Seattle, Washington: *zoo.org*

- **Zoo Miami,** Miami, Florida: *zoomiami.org*

Canada

- **Assiniboine Park Zoo,** Winnipeg, Manitoba: *assiniboinepark.ca*

- **British Columbia Wildlife Park,** Kamloops, British Columbia: *bcwildlife.org*

- **Calgary Zoo,** Calgary, Alberta: *calgaryzoo.com*

- **Toronto Zoo,** Toronto, Ontario: *torontozoo.com*

- **Vancouver Aquarium,** Vancouver, British Columbia: *vanaqua.org*

Mexico, Central and South America

- **Africam Safari,** Puebla, Mexico: *africamsafari.com*

- **Buin Zoo,** Buin, Chile: *buinzoo.cl*

- **São Paulo Zoo,** São Paulo, Brazil: *zoologico.com.br*

Europe

- **Copenhagen Zoo,** Copenhagen, Denmark: *zoo.dk*

- **Dublin Zoo,** Dublin, Ireland: *dublinzoo.ie*

- **London Zoo,** London, England: *zsl.org/zsl-london-zoo*

- **Parc Zoologique de Paris,** Paris, France: *parczoologiquedeparis.fr/en*

- **Tiergarten Schönbrunn,** Vienna, Austria: *zoovienna.at*

- **Zoologischer Garten Berlin,** Berlin, Germany: *nzpnewdelhi.gov.in*

Asia

- **National Zoological Park,** New Delhi, India: *nzpnewdelhi.gov.in*

- **Singapore Zoo,** Singapore: *zoo.com.sg*

- **Zoo Negara,** Ampang, Malaysia: *zoonegaramalaysia.my*

Africa

- **National Zoological Gardens of South Africa,** Pretoria, South Africa: *nzg.ac.za*

- **The South African Association for Marine Biological Research,** Durban, South Africa: *seaworld.org.za*

Australia

- **Adelaide Zoo,** Adelaide, South Australia: *adelaidezoo.com.au*

- **Perth Zoo,** Perth, Western Australia: *perthzoo.wa.gov.au*

INDEX

267

PHOTO & ILLUSTRATION CREDITS

FRONT COVER: (snake), Am Wu/iStockphoto; (bald eagle), Sekar B/Shutterstock; (fish), Dan Huertas/Icon Films/Caters News Agency; (spider), Henrik Larsson/Shutterstock; (wolf), Jeff Vanuga/Corbis RM Stills/Getty Images; (shark), Daniela Dirscherl/WaterFrame RM/Getty Images; **SPINE:** (lion), Eric Isselée/Shutterstock; (fish), Dan Huertas/Icon Films/Caters News Agency; **BACK COVER:** (owl), Medvedev Vladimir/Shutterstock; (leopard), Eric Isselée/iStockphoto/Getty Images; **BACK FLAP:** (author), Jackie Phairow; (spider), Karolina Chaberek/Shutterstock

VARIOUS THROUGHOUT: (bird feather background), Boonchuay Promjiam/Shutterstock; (coral pattern background), joesayhello/Shutterstock; (fish scales background), Kevin H Knuth/Shutterstock; (sheep fur background), majeczka/Shutterstock; (chameleon skin close-up), xlt974/Shutterstock; (zebra fur background), Photodisc

FRONT MATTER: 1, MogensTrolle/iStockphoto/Getty Images; 2 (UP), Andrew Burgess/Shutterstock; 2 (CTR RT), Gérard Soury/Biosphoto; 2 (CTR LE), Arto Hakola/Shutterstock; 2 (LO LE), Bianca Lavies/National Geographic Creative; 2 (LO RT), blickwinkel/Alamy Stock Photo; 3 (UP), Solvin Zank/Nature Picture Library; 3 (CTR RT), Marc_Latremouille/iStockphoto/Getty Images; 3 (LO), Jalen Evans/EyeEm/Getty Images; 4 (UP), Robert L Kothenbeutel/Shutterstock; 4 (LO), Borut Furlan/WaterFrame RM/Getty Images; 5, Andreanita/Dreamstime; 6, Jackie Phairow; 7, Patrick Greene

DISCOVERING PREDATORS: 8-9, AOosthuizen/iStockphoto/Getty Images; 10 (LO), Flip Nicklin/National Geographic Creative; 10-11, Solvin Zankl/Nature Picture Library; 11 (UP LE), Michael Quinton/Minden Pictures; 11 (UP RT), Joanne Weston/Shutterstock; 11 (CTR), Michael and Patricia Fogden/Minden Pictures; 11 (LO), Nigel Cattlin/Alamy Stock Photo; 12, schubbel/Shutterstock; 13 (UP), Ludmila Yilmaz/Shutterstock; 13 (CTR RT), Dietmar Nill/Nature Picture Library; 13 (LO), Wang LiQiang/Shutterstock; 14, David Haring/DUPC/Getty Images; 15 (UP), Paul Souders/Corbis Documentary/Getty Images; 15 (CTR RT), Scott Camazine/Alamy Stock Photo; 15 (LO LE), Marek Stefunko/Alamy Stock Photo; 16 (UP), Jason Prince/Dreamstime; 16 (CTR), PHOTOCREO Michal Bednarek/Shutterstock; 16 (LO), Maggy Meyer/Shutterstock; 17 (Harris's hawk), Pavel Mikoska/Shutterstock; 17 (coyote), Warren Metcalf/Shutterstock; 17 (kingsnake), Matt Jeppson/Shutterstock; 17 (desert tortoise), Matt Jeppson/Shutterstock; 17 (kangaroo rat), Been there YB/Shutterstock; 17 (white-winged dove), Martha Marks/Shutterstock; 17 (Gila woodpecker), digidreamgrafix/Shutterstock; 17 (harvester ant), Pavel Krasensky/Shutterstock; 17 (saguaro cactus), Bill Florence/Shutterstock; 18-19, Barrett Hedges/National Geographic Creative; 19 (UP LE), Brian J. Skerry/National Geographic Creative; 19 (UP RT), Frans Lanting/Geographic Creative; 20, KEENPRESS/National Geographic Creative; 21 (UP LE), Alex Mustard/2020VISION/NPL/Minden Pictures; 21 (UP RT), Nick Upton/NPL/Minden Pictures; 21 (LO), BrianEKushner/iStockphoto/Getty Images; 22 (LO LE), Brent Paull Photography; 22 (LO RT), Roland Seitre/Nature Picture Library; 23 (UP), Georgette Douwma/Nature Picture Library; 23 (LO RT), FLPA/Minden Pictures; 24, Australian Scenics/Photolibrary RM/

Getty Images; 25 (UP LE), Andrew Skolnick/Shutterstock; 25 (UP RT), R Hansen Richard/Science Source/Getty Images; 25 (LO), Melanie Wynarski/EyeEm/Getty Images; 26, Franco Tempesta; 27 (UP LE), Franco Tempesta; 27 (UP RT), Franco Tempesta; 27 (CTR), Kostyantyn Ivanyshen/Shutterstock; 27 (LO RT), Franco Tempesta; 28 (LO LE), Reimar/Alamy Stock Photo; 28-29, altrendo nature/Getty Images; 29 (UP RT), David Tipling/Biosphoto; 29 (CTR RT), Berndt Fischer/Oxford Scientific RM/Getty Images; 29 (LO LE), Danita Delimont/Gallo Images/Getty Images; 30 (LO LE), Brian J. Skerry/National Geographic Creative; 30-31, Martin Strmiska/Alamy Stock Photo; 31 (UP RT), Tony Wu/Nature Picture Library; 31 (CTR RT), Westend61/Getty Images; 31 (LO), Matthias Breiter/Minden Pictures; 32 (LO LE), Andrew M. Snyder/Moment RF/Getty Images; 32-33, age fotostock/Alamy Stock Photo; 33 (UP RT), Chien Lee/Minden Pictures; 33 (CTR RT), Rob Jordan/2020VISION/Nature Picture Library; 33 (LO LE), Ian Butler Bird/Alamy Stock Photo; 34, Klein & Hubert/Nature Picture Library; 35 (CTR), Martin Moos/Lonely Planet Images/Getty Images; 35 (inset), Wim van den Heever/Nature Picture Library; 35 (LO RT), Marcus Westberg; 36, Chris Hill/Shutterstock; 37 (UP LE), Otto Plantema/Buitenbeeld/Minden Pictures; 37 (CTR RT), Andreanita/Dreamstime; 37 (LO), Volodymyr Byrdyak/Dreamstime; 38 (LO RT), Pniesen/Dreamstime; 39 (UP), FloridaStock/Shutterstock; 39 (LO), Christian Vinces/Shutterstock

FANGS, CLAWS & GAPING JAWS: PREDATORY MAMMALS: 40-41, Bruno Pambour/Biosphoto; 42-43, Kristina Perlerius/iStockphoto; 43 (UP LE), Bob Smith/National Geographic Creative; 43 (UP RT), Tui De Roy/Minden Pictures; 43 (CTR RT), Stefan Greif/National Geographic Creative; 43 (LO LE), Paul Nicklen/National Geographic Creative; 43 (LO RT), Kirsten Wahlquist/Shutterstock; 44, AndreAnita/iStockphoto/Getty Images; 45, G Ribiere/Shutterstock; 46, Andy Rouse/Nature Picture Library; 47, Aditya Dicky Singh/Alamy Stock Photo; 48, Beverly Joubert/National Geographic Creative; 49, Nikita Gusak/iStockphoto/Getty Images; 50, Jeannette Katzir Photog/Shutterstock; 51, Stayer/Shutterstock; 52, Kenneth Geiger/National Geographic Creative; 53, skilpad/iStockphoto/Getty Images; 54, Jak Wonderly/NGP; 55, Nick Dale/iStockphoto/Getty Images; 56, Dennis Donohue/Dreamstime; 57, Moose Henderson/Dreamstime; 58, Magdanatka/Shutterstock; 59, Byrdyak/iStockphoto/Getty Images; 60, AndreAnita/iStockphoto/Getty Images; 61, Don Johnston_MA/Alamy Stock Photo; 62, Outdoorsman/Dreamstime; 63, Geoffrey Kuchera/Shutterstock; 64, Eric Gevaert/Shutterstock; 65, Beverly Joubert/National Geographic Creative; 66, Peter Chadwick/Gallo Images/Getty Images; 67, Richard Packwood/Photodisc/Getty Images; 68, Valentyna Chukhlyebova/Shutterstock; 69, Jason Edwards/National Geographic Creative; 70, David Pattyn/Nature Picture Library; 71, cameglio/iStockphoto/Getty Images; 72, Flip Nicklin/National Geographic Creative; 73, Patricio Robles Gil/Minden Pictures; 74, Gleb Tarro/Shutterstock; 75, rpbirdman/iStockphoto/Getty Images; 76, Hemis/Alamy Stock Photo; 77, Axel Gomille/Nature Picture Library; 78, Anup Shah/Nature Picture Library; 79, Danny Alvarez/Shutterstock; 80, Martin Harvey/Gallo Images/Getty Images; 81, Beverly Joubert/National Geographic Creative; 82, Des & Jen Bartlett/National Geographic

CREDITS

The publisher would like to thank everyone who worked to make this book come together: Priyanka Lamichhane, senior editor; Sanjida Rashid, art director; Lori Epstein, photo director; Susan Bishansky, project editor and manager; Michelle Harris, fact-checker

Since 1888, the National Geographic Society has funded more than 12,000 research, exploration, and preservation projects around the world. The Society receives funds from National Geographic Partners, LLC, funded in part by your purchase. A portion of the proceeds from this book supports this vital work. To learn more, visit natgeo.com/info.

For more information, visit nationalgeographic .com, call 1-800-647-5463, or write to the following address:

National Geographic Partners
1145 17th Street N.W.
Washington, D.C. 20036-4688 U.S.A.

Visit us online at nationalgeographic.com/books

For librarians and teachers: ngchildrensbooks.org

More for kids from National Geographic: natgeokids.com

For information about special discounts for bulk purchases, please contact National Geographic Books Special Sales: specialsales@natgeo.com

For rights or permissions inquiries, please contact National Geographic Books Subsidiary Rights: bookrights@natgeo.com

Designed by Angela Terry and Sanjida Rashid

Hardcover ISBN: 978-1-4263-3178-7
Reinforced library binding ISBN:
978-1-4263-3179-4

Printed in China
18/RRDS/1